Collins

INTERNATIONAL
PRIMARY
MATHS

Student's Book 3

William Collins' dream of knowledge for all began with the publication of his first book in 1819.
A self-educated mill worker, he not only enriched millions of lives, but also founded a flourishing publishing house. Today, staying true to this spirit, Collins books are packed with inspiration, innovation and practical expertise. They place you at the centre of a world of possibility and give you exactly what you need to explore it.

Collins. Freedom to teach.

An imprint of HarperCollins*Publishers*
The News Building
1 London Bridge Street
London
SE1 9GF

Browse the complete Collins catalogue at www.collins.co.uk

10 9 8 7

ISBN 978-0-00-815989-4

British Library Cataloguing in Publication Data
A catalogue record for this publication is available from the British Library.

Commissioned by Fiona McGlade
Series editor Peter Clarke
Project editor Kate Ellis
Project managed by Emily Hooton
Developed by Joan Miller, Tracy Thomas and Karen Williams
Edited by Catherine Dakin
Proofread by Catherine Dakin
Cover design by Ink Tank
Cover artwork by Jose Lis Petaez/Getty Images
Internal design by Ken Vail Graphic Design
Typesetting by Ken Vail Graphic Design
Illustrations by Ken Vail Graphic Design, Advocate Art and Beehive Illustrations
Production by Lauren Crisp

Printed and bound by Grafica Veneta S. P. A.

Contents

Number

1 Whole numbers 1   1

2 Whole numbers 2   9

3 Whole numbers 3   17

4 Fractions   21

5 Addition and subtraction 1   29

6 Addition and subtraction 2   37

7 Addition and subtraction 3   45

8 Multiplication and division 1   53

9 Multiplication and division 2   61

10 Multiplication and division 3   69

Geometry

11 2D shape   77

12 3D shape   81

13 Position and movement   85

Measure

14 Money   93

15 Length   97

16 Mass   101

17 Capacity   105

18 Time   109

Handling Data

19 Organising, categorising and representing data   113

Lesson 1: **Reading and writing numbers**

Number

- Count to 200 and beyond
- Read and write numbers to 1000

Discover

Numbers are all around you. They can help you put things in order, or count objects.

Learn

Numbers can be written in words and in numerals. It is quicker to read a number in numerals, so most numbers are written in this way. The house numbers above are written in numerals.

Example

= four hundred and sixty five = 465

= two hundred and three = 203

Number

Lesson 2: Counting on and back in steps (1)

- Count on and back in 1s, 10s and 100s

Discover

When you first learn to count, you count in 1s. Then you learn to count in 10s and 100s. Counting in 100s, 10s and 1s can help you count large amounts quickly.

Learn

The digits in a 3-digit number are worth 100s, 10s and 1, so when we count in 100s, 10s or 1s, that particular digit changes.

Example

Look carefully at these examples, starting with the number 378:

Counting in 1s	Counting in 10s	Counting in 100s
378	378	378
379	388	478
380	398	578
381	408	678

Look down each column. What do you notice about how the numbers change?

Lesson 3: **Counting on and back in steps (2)**

Key words
• forwards (on)
• backwards (back)

- Count forwards and backwards in 2s, 3s, 4s and 5s

Number

Discover

When objects come in groups, it can be quicker to count them in 2s, 3s, 4s or 5s.

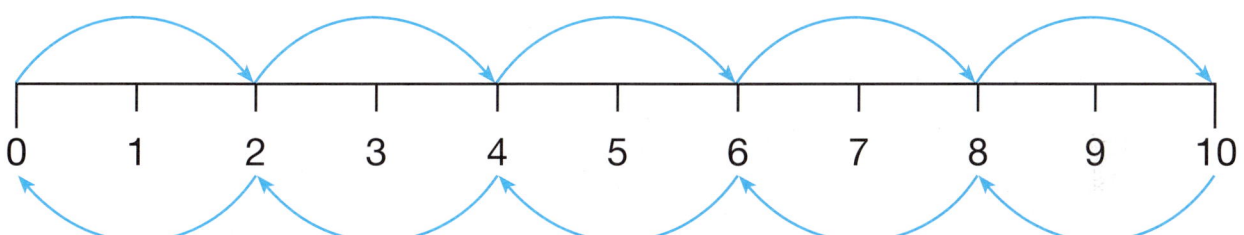

Learn

When counting in steps of the same number, there are often patterns you can spot to help you.

Using a 100 square is a useful way to identify these patterns and help you step count.

1	2	3	4	5	6	7	8	9	10
11	12	13	14	15	16	17	18	19	20
21	22	23	24	25	26	27	28	29	30
31	32	33	34	35	36	37	38	39	40
41	42	43	44	45	46	47	48	49	50
51	52	53	54	55	56	57	58	59	60
61	62	63	64	65	66	67	68	69	70
71	72	73	74	75	76	77	78	79	80
81	82	83	84	85	86	87	88	89	90
91	92	93	94	95	96	97	98	99	100

Example

Count in steps of 2: 2, 4, 6, 8, 10, ... Look at the blue boxes in the 100 square.

Count in steps of 3: 3, 6, 9, 12, 15, ...

Count in steps of 4: 4, 8, 12, 16, 20, ...

Count in steps of 5: 5, 10, 15, 20, 25, ... Look at the red boxes in the 100 square.

Lesson 4: **Place value (1)**

Number

- Recognise the value of each digit in a 3-digit number

Discover

Hundreds, tens and ones (or units) are building blocks that help you to write numbers.

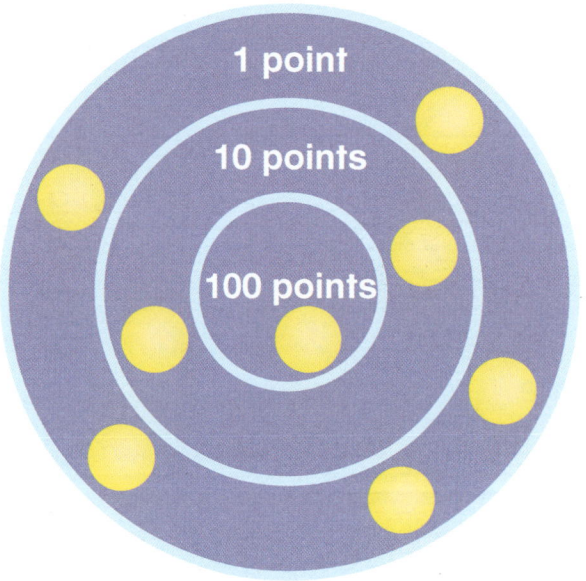

1 point

10 points

100 points

> The position of a digit in a number affects its value.

Learn

3-digit numbers are made up of hundreds, tens and units. The number 573 contains 5 hundreds (500), 7 tens (70) and 3 units (3).

Example

Hundreds	Tens	Units
2	5	8
8	6	1

In 258, the 8 is worth 8 units or ones.
In 861, the 8 is worth 8 hundreds.

Lesson 5: **Place value (2)**

- Recognise the value of each digit in a 3-digit number
- Partition 3-digit numbers into hundreds, tens and units

Key words
- value
- hundreds
- tens
- ones/units

Discover

Each digit in a 3-digit number is worth an amount of ones, tens or hundreds, depending where it is written.

300   **10**   **4**

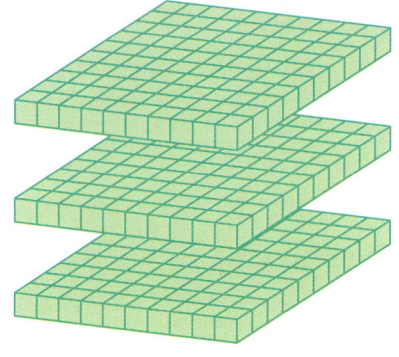   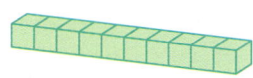

Learn

A 3-digit number can be split into hundreds, tens and units. You can write the number shown by the peas on the fork as 314, but also as 300 + 10 + 4.

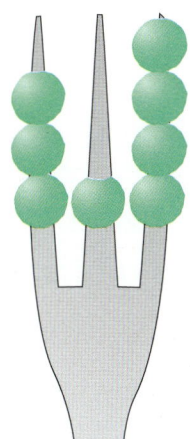

Example
673 = 600 + 70 + 3
294 = 200 + 90 + 4

Lesson 6: **1, 10, 100 more or less (1)**

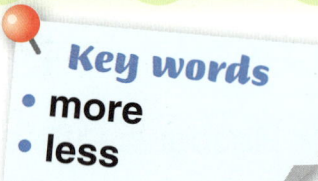

Key words
• more
• less

• Find 1, 10 or 100 more or less than a number

Discover

This is part of a number square. You can use number squares to help you count in 1s and 10s.

```
        235
244  245  246
        255
```

```
         (blue)
(orange)  632  (red)
         (yellow)
```

Learn

3-digit numbers are made up of hundreds, tens and units. If they change by 100, 10 or 1, the hundreds, tens or units digit will change by 1. Sometimes, two digits will change.

Example

What number is 100 more than 512?   6̲12

What number is 10 less than 439?   42̲9

Look how **two digits** change in the next example.
What number is 1 more than 679?   6̲8̲0̲

Lesson 7: **Marking numbers on a number line (1)**

- Place 3-digit numbers correctly on a number line marked in multiples of 100

Key words
- more
- less
- between
- multiple of 100

Number

Discover

Numbers belong in order. At first, you used a number line from 1 to 10. Now you will look at number lines for 3-digit numbers.

Learn

Every 3-digit number that isn't a multiple of 100 lies between two multiples of 100 – one that is smaller and one that is larger.

Each number's position can be shown on a number line.

Example
Mark 418 on the number line.
418 is between 400 and 500, but closer to 400.
Its position can be marked like this.

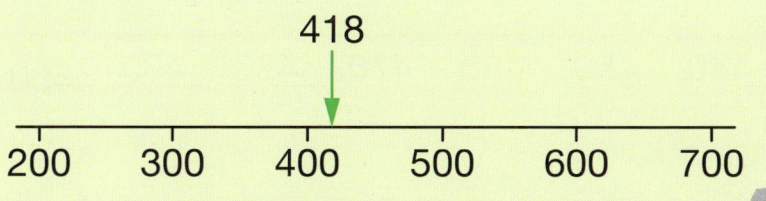

Lesson 8: **Marking numbers on a number line (2)**

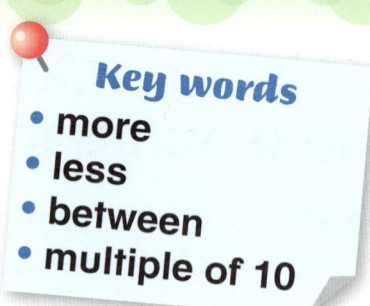

Key words
- more
- less
- between
- multiple of 10

- Place 3-digit numbers correctly on a number line marked in 10s

Number

Discover

Every whole number can be written on a number line.
This one shows where 3-digit numbers belong.

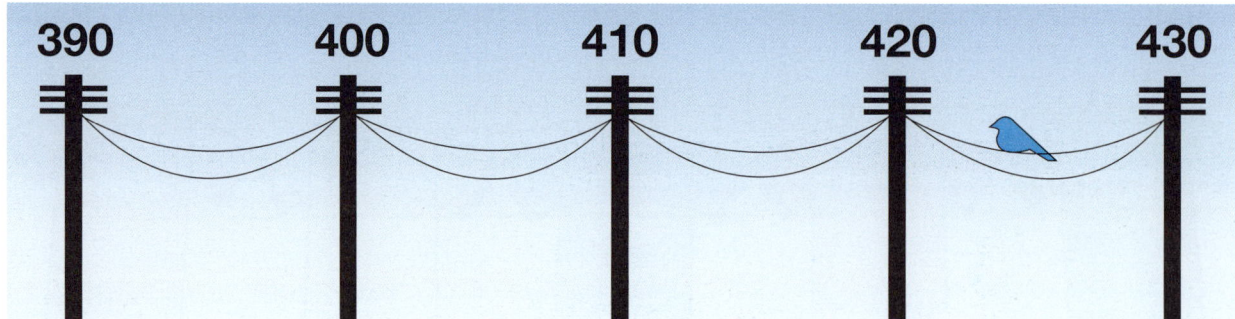

390   400   410   420   430

Learn

In Lesson 7, you learned how to place numbers on a number line split into 100s. If the number line is split into 10s, you can place numbers more accurately.

Example

Where does 418 go on the number line?

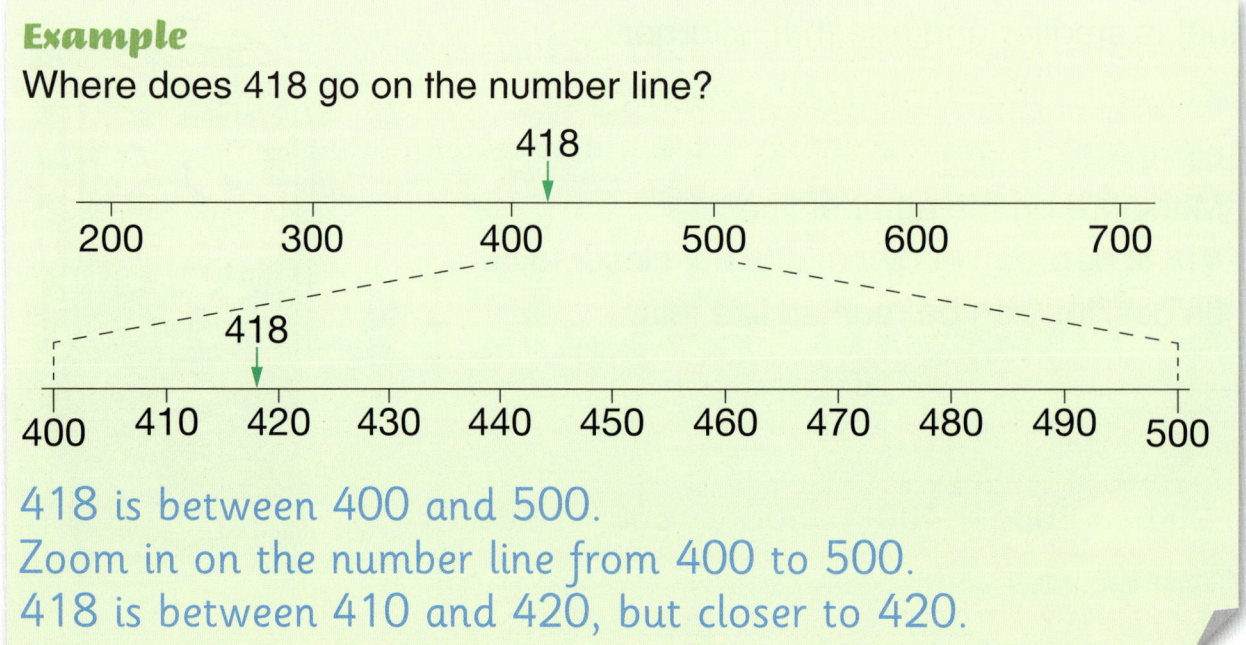

418 is between 400 and 500.
Zoom in on the number line from 400 to 500.
418 is between 410 and 420, but closer to 420.

Lesson 1: **Counting on and back in steps (3)**

Key words
- forwards (on)
- backwards (back)

- Count on and back in different-sized steps

Discover

Counting in steps is a quick way of getting from one number to another.

Learn

Counting in steps is like a frog jumping forwards or backwards the same distance every time.

Sometimes there are patterns in the numbers that can help.

Example
Counting on in 5s:

20   25   30   35

Counting back in 10s:

46   36   26   16

9

Lesson 2: **Place value (3)**

- Know the value of each digit in a 3-digit number

Discover

Each type of Base 10 block has a different value.

Learn

The digits in 3-digit numbers are worth hundreds, tens and units. The value of a digit depends on its position in the number.

Example

The digit 3 in the number 637 is worth 3 tens or 30.

The digit 3 in the number 329 is worth 3 hundreds or 300.

6	3	7

6 0 0	3 0	7

3	2	9

3 0 0	2 0	9

Number

Lesson 3: **1, 10, 100 more or less (2)**

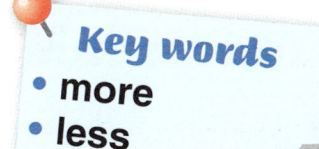

Key words
- more
- less

- Find 1, 10 or 100 more or less than a number

Discover

Counting forwards or backwards in 1s, 10s or 100s is a quick way of counting.

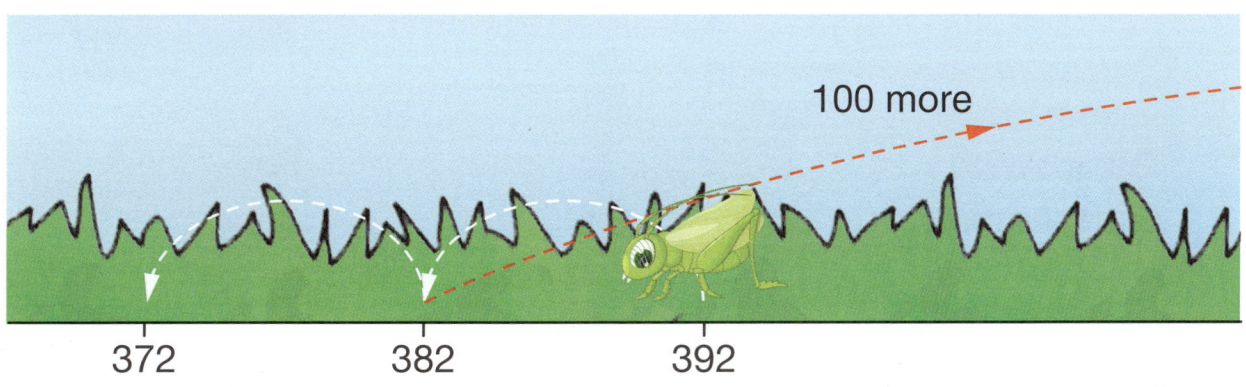

100 more

372   382   392

Learn

The digits, from left to right, in a 3-digit number are worth hundreds, tens or ones.

When numbers increase or decrease by 100, 10 or 1, it is that particular digit that changes by one.

Example

100 less than:	9	3	2
is:	8	3	2
1 more than:	5	0	1
is:	5	0	2

Notice that two digits change here:

10 less than:	2	0	2
is:	1	9	2

Look at the digits that change.

Number

Lesson 4: **Multiplying by 10 (1)**

• Multiply 2-digit numbers by 10

Key words
• multiply
• multiple
• place value

Discover

Multiplying numbers doesn't always change the digits. When you multiply a number by 10, the digits just move left.

H   T   U

7   8

H   T   U

7   8   0

Learn

When a number is multiplied by 10, its digits shift one place to the left, just like the 7 and the 8 shuffling up on the bench in the picture. To show this, we use a zero in the empty units column.

Example

H	T	U
	3	4
3	4	0

$34 \times 10 = 340$

12

Lesson 5: **Rounding**

- Round 2-digit and 3-digit numbers

Discover

You can round a number to give a close estimate.

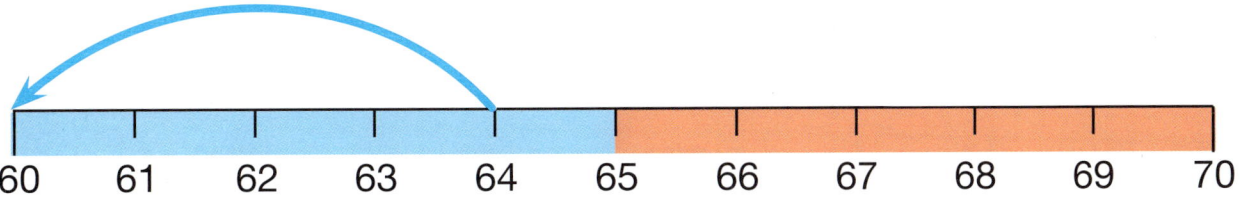

Learn

Maths sometimes involves numbers that are not exact.
You can round numbers to the nearest 10 or 100.

To round 2-digit numbers to the nearest 10, look at the UNIT.
If the unit is 0, 1, 2, 3 or 4, round down.
If the unit is 5, 6, 7, 8 or 9, round up.

To round 3-digit numbers to the nearest 100 look at the TEN.
If the ten is 0, 1, 2, 3 or 4, round down.
If the ten is 5, 6, 7, 8 or 9, round up.

Example

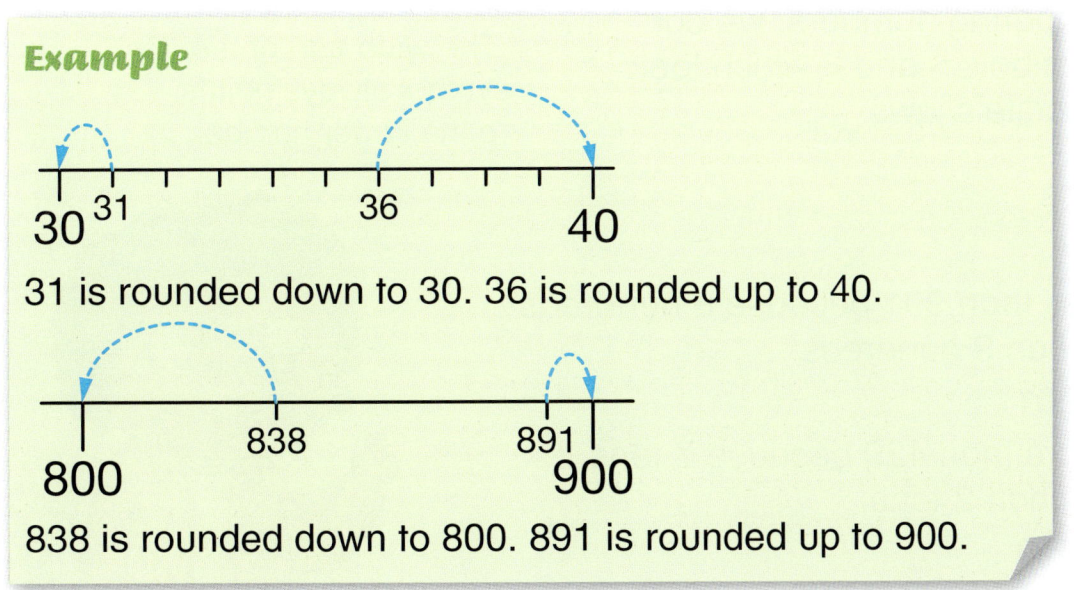

31 is rounded down to 30. 36 is rounded up to 40.

838 is rounded down to 800. 891 is rounded up to 900.

Number

Lesson 6: **Comparing numbers (1)**

• Use > and < signs to compare 3-digit numbers

Discover

The shape of this crocodile's mouth is like a 'less than' sign.

Learn

When comparing numbers, we can use the symbols > and < which look like a crocodile's jaws.

The wide part of the symbol always points to the larger number.

Example

839 is less than 901 because 8 hundreds are less than 9 hundreds:

  839 < 901

471 is more than 429 because 7 tens are more than 2 tens:

  471 > 429

Lesson 7: **Ordering numbers (1)**

- Order 2- and 3-digit numbers

Discover

You can use the fact that numbers belong in an order to help you put other things in order.

Learn

When you order numbers, you use exactly the same skill as when you compare them.

a Look at the number of digits in the numbers.

b Then compare the values of the digits, from left to right.

Example

Compare and order these numbers.

    371   47   289

a 47 only has two digits so it is the smallest number.

b 371 has more hundreds than 289, so the order from largest to smallest is 371, 289, 47.

Lesson 8: **Estimating**

- Estimate numbers as a range

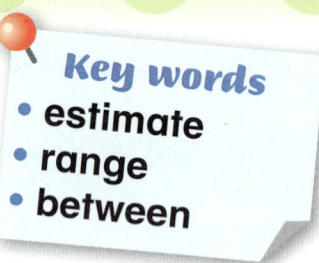

Number

Discover

Maths in everyday life is not always based on exact numbers or calculations. It may be based on **estimates**.

Learn

An estimate is a sensible guess. If you estimate that there are 80 people in your class, this is not a sensible guess!

Example

How many people are there in this picture?

a Estimate a range: 20 to 30

b Group into tens:

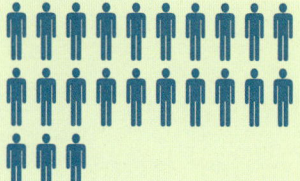

c Count and check: 23 people ✓

Lesson 1: **Multiplying by 10 (2)**

• Multiply 2-digit numbers by 10

Key words
• multiply
• multiple
• place value

Number

Discover

Multiplying a number by 10 pushes its digits to the left.

Learn

When 27 is multiplied by 10, the digits move along one place, as if the digits have changed lanes in the swimming pool. The zero is needed to show that the units place is now empty, so 27 becomes 270.

Example
$53 \times 10 = 530$

17

Number

Lesson 2: **Estimating and rounding**

- Estimate and round numbers

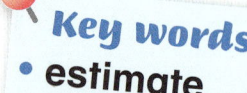

Key words
- estimate
- range
- between
- round
- multiple

Discover

In everyday life, it is often important to make a good guess or to round numbers to make them simpler to use.

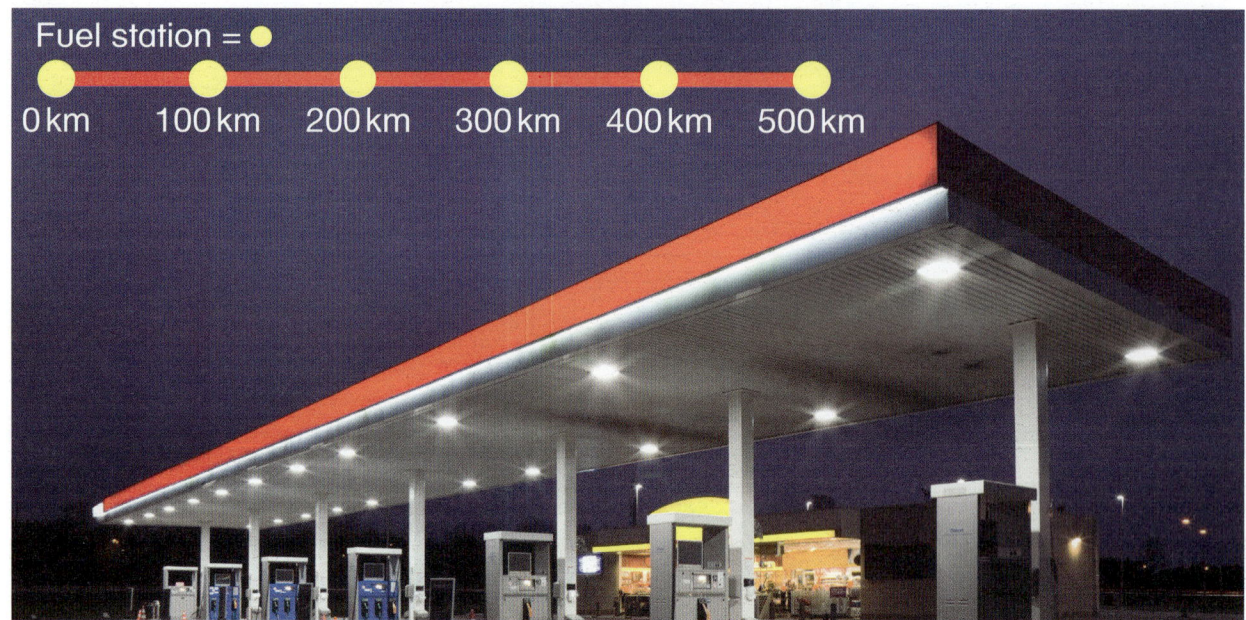

Fuel station = ●

0 km   100 km   200 km   300 km   400 km   500 km

Learn

You are practising two skills – **estimating** and **rounding**.

When you estimate an amount, or a number, you make a sensible guess about how big it is.
When you round a number, you make it easier to work with by changing it to the nearest 10 or 100.

Example

Estimate the number of bicycles in a bike shop as a range.

I estimate there are 30 – 40 bicycles.
Sort into groups of 10:

Count to check estimate: 35 ✓
Round to the nearest 10: 40

Lesson 3: **Comparing numbers (2)**

- Compare 3-digit numbers using > and < signs

Discover

It is often important to know which number is larger or smaller than another one.

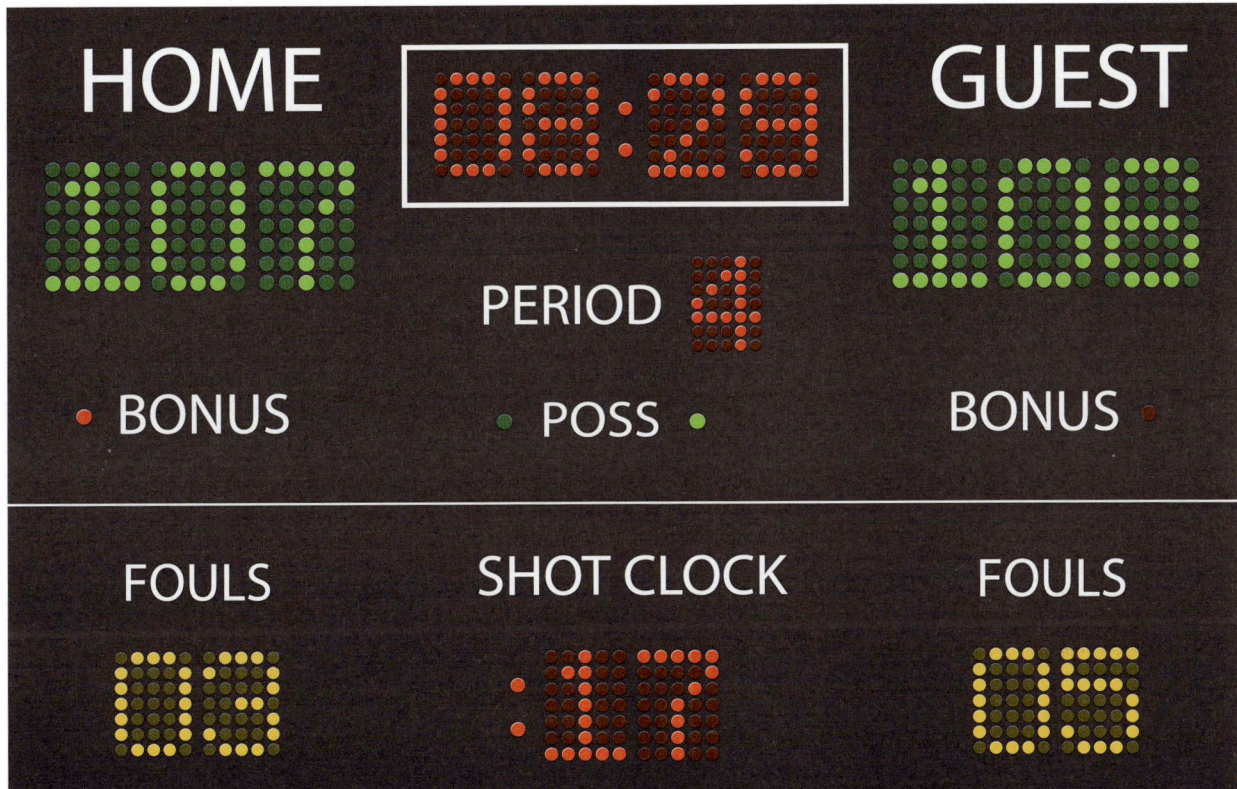

Learn

When comparing two numbers, it is important to look at the digits that are worth the most first.

Example

Which is larger, 611 or 399?

6 hundreds are more than 3 hundreds, so 611 > 399.

Which is larger, 752 or 781?

The hundreds are the same, but 5 tens are less than 8 tens, so 752 < 781.

Number

Number

Lesson 4: **Ordering numbers (2)**

• Order 2- and 3-digit numbers

Discover
Numbers belong in order.

302   159   270   29   184

Learn
Placing numbers in order means making sure that they are written from smallest to largest, or largest to smallest.

The best way to do this is to look carefully at each digit from left to right and compare them.

Example
259, 257, 159
from smallest to largest is 159, 257, 259
637, 742, 628
from largest to smallest is 742, 637, 628

Lesson 1: **Finding half**

- Find half of numbers up to 40

📌 **Key words**
- half
- odd
- even

Discover

Sometimes you need to share something into 2 equal parts.

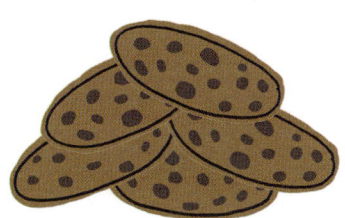

Learn

Finding half of a number is the same as splitting it into 2 equal parts.

Sometimes those parts are whole numbers.

Sometimes those parts end in $\frac{1}{2}$.

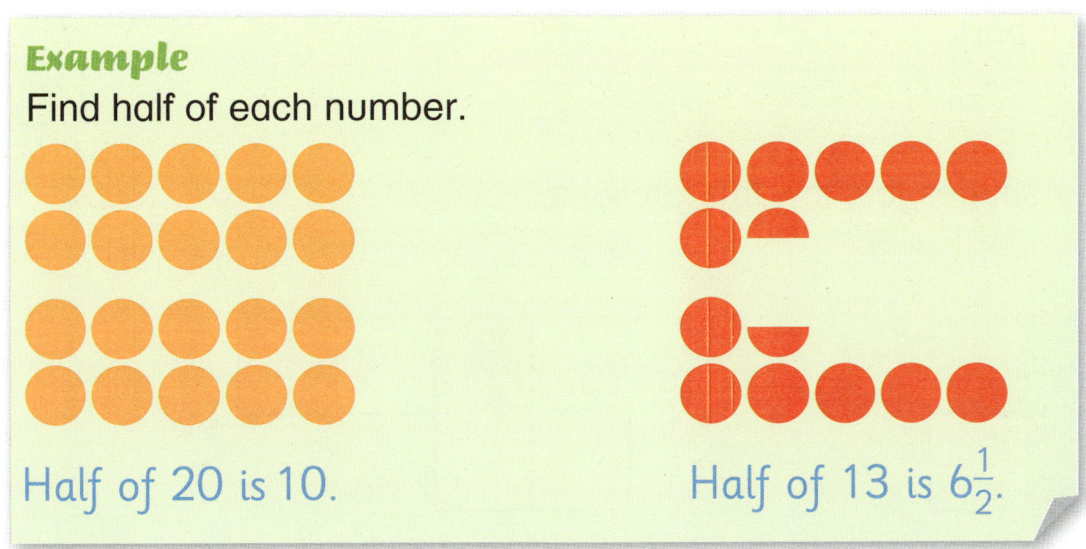

Example

Find half of each number.

Half of 20 is 10.

Half of 13 is $6\frac{1}{2}$.

21

Number

Lesson 2: **Non-unitary fractions**

- Write fractions correctly
- Understand that fractions can show more than one part

Key words
- **numerator**
- **denominator**
- **part**
- **whole**

Discover

Learn

Fractions show parts of a whole.

The top number (**numerator**) shows how many chosen parts there are. The bottom number (**denominator**) shows how many there are altogether. $\frac{1}{4}$ is 1 out of a possible 4 parts.

Unitary means 1, so **non-unitary** fractions are fractions with more than 1 part.

Example
Shade the shapes to show the fractions.

a $\frac{3}{4}$

$\frac{3}{4}$

b $\frac{2}{5}$

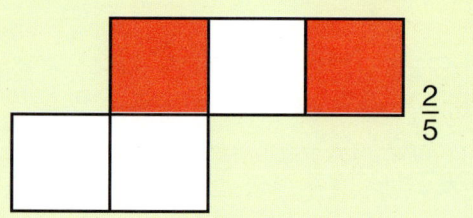

$\frac{2}{5}$

Lesson 3: **Equivalent fractions**

- Recognise fractions that are worth the same

Key words
- equivalent
- equal
- half

Discover

How many ways can you cut the pizza in half?

Learn

Equivalent fractions are fractions that look different – they have different numbers and a different number of parts, but they are worth the same.

Example

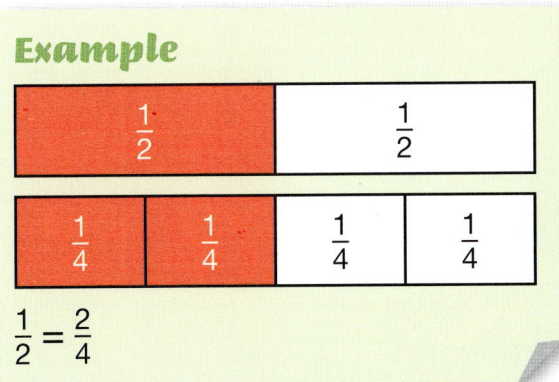

$\frac{1}{2} = \frac{2}{4}$

Lesson 4: **Mixed fractions**

• Recognise simple mixed fractions

Key words
• mixed fraction
• whole number
• fraction

Discover

How many bricks are in each strip?

Learn

A mixed fraction, also called a mixed number, is made up of a whole number and a fraction. The painted strips in the picture show some whole bricks with part of a brick (a fraction) on the end.

Example

How many glasses of milk are there?

whole number   fraction

There are $3\frac{1}{2}$ glasses of milk – a mixed fraction.

Number

Lesson 5: **Ordering fractions**

- Order fractions or mixed fractions on a number line

Key words
- **more than**
- **less than**
- **mixed fraction**
- **between**

Number

Discover

Fractions are numbers, so they can be shown on a number line.

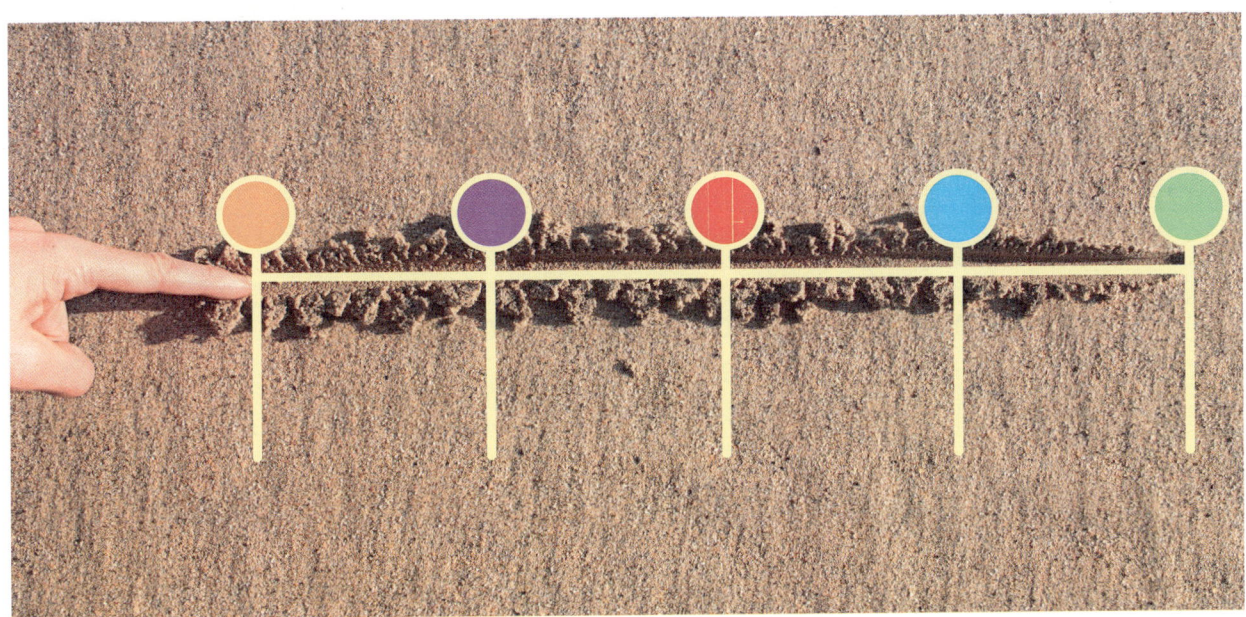

Learn

Simple fractions ($\frac{1}{2}$, $\frac{3}{4}$, ...) and mixed fractions ($3\frac{1}{4}$, $5\frac{1}{2}$, ...) lie between whole numbers.

Each is more than one whole number, but less than the next whole number.

$6\frac{1}{2}$ is more than 6, but it is less than 7.

Example

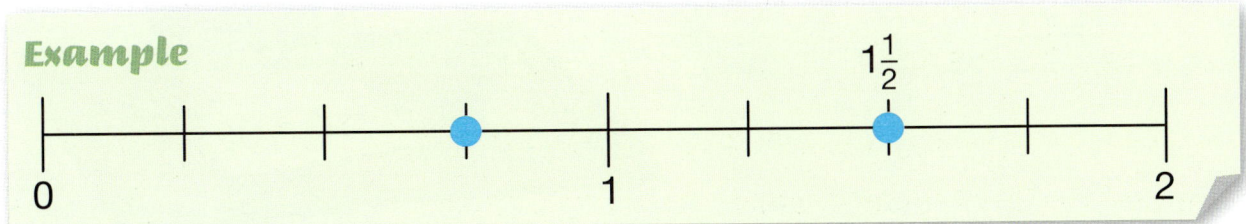

Number

Lesson 6: **Fractions and division**

Key words
- **fraction**
- **divide**

- Understand how finding fractions is linked to division

Discover

As well as **finding half**, what other words can you use to describe what you need to do here?

Learn

Finding a fraction of a number is the same as dividing that number. For example, when you find $\frac{1}{2}$ of a number, it is the same as dividing by 2.

Example

$$\frac{1}{2} \text{ of } 40 = 40 \div 2$$
$$= 20$$

$$\frac{1}{10} \text{ of } 30 = 30 \div 10$$
$$= 3$$

Lesson 7: **Finding fractions of shapes**

- Find halves, thirds, quarters and tenths of shapes

Discover

Learn

Shapes can be split into fractions as long as each part is the same size.

Think of each fraction as the number of parts you have, out of the total possible parts of the shape.

Example

A

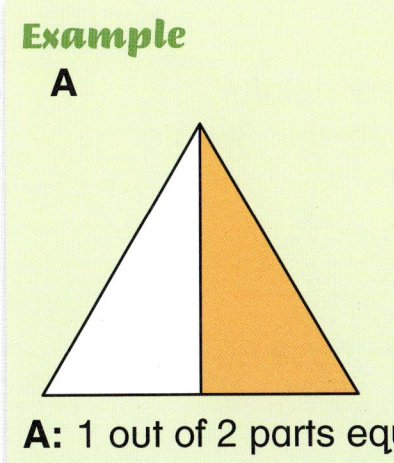

B

A: 1 out of 2 parts equals $\frac{1}{2}$ **B:** 3 out of 4 parts equals $\frac{3}{4}$

27

Number

Lesson 8: **Finding fractions of numbers**

- Find halves, thirds, quarters and tenths of numbers

Discover

Fractions are often used by shops to show changes in prices. A half-price sale means that the price of everything is halved.

$26

Now $\frac{1}{2}$ price!

$12

Now only $\frac{1}{4}$ the price!

Learn

When finding a fraction of a number, division is very helpful. For example, if you want to find $\frac{1}{2}$ of 36, you need to split 36 into 2 equal parts – divide it by 2.

Example

$\frac{1}{4}$ of 12 = 3 because 12 ÷ 4 = 3 $\frac{1}{10}$ of 80 = 8 because 80 ÷ 10 = 8

$\frac{1}{2}$ of 36 = 18 because 36 ÷ 2 = 18

Lesson 1: **Addition and subtraction facts to 20**

- Know addition and subtraction facts for numbers to 20

Discover

Numbers bond in pairs to make a total.
The apples on the trees total 17 (12 + 5).

Learn

Addition means combining numbers together. Other terms that mean **add** are **plus**, **total** and **find the sum of**.

Subtraction means taking one number away from another. Other terms that mean **subtract** are **minus**, **take away** and **find the difference between**.

Example
Find the sum of 7 and 9.
$7 + 9 = 16$
What is 3 less than 15?
$15 - 3 = 12$

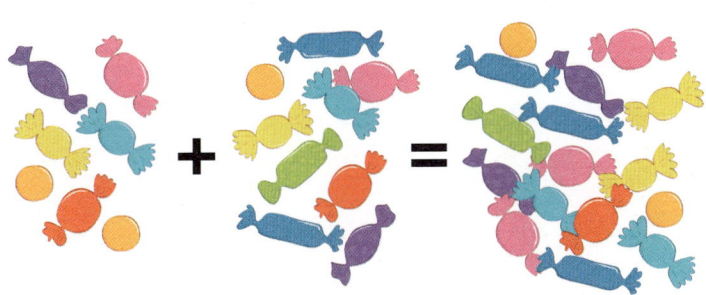

Number

Lesson 2: **Multiples of 100 that total 1000**

Key words
• multiple of 100
• total

• Identify multiples of 100 with a total of 1000

Discover

Multiples of 100 that make totals of 1000.

 4 +  6 =  10

 40 +  60 =  ?

 ? + 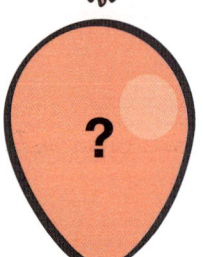 ? =  ?

Learn

When you are adding multiples of 100 to make a total of 1000, you need to know the numbers that make 10. If you know these, you can use them to help because 100 lots of 10 are 1000.

Example

2 + 8 = 10

So 200 + 800 = 1000

7 + 3 = 10

So 700 + 300 = 1000

Lesson 3: **Multiples of 5 that total 100**

• Identify multiples of 5 with a total of 100

Key words
• multiple of 5
• multiple of 10
• total

Discover

Multiples of 5 can make number bonds for 100.

Learn

Count in 5s. Do you see the pattern?

5, 1**0**, 1**5**, 2**0**, 2**5**, 3**0**

It is possible to make 100 by adding some of these multiples of 5.

Example

If you know pairs that make 10, it will help you find pairs that end in 0 and make 100.

$6 + 4 = 10$

So $60 + 40 = 100$

Now find a pair that both end in 5.

$35 + 65 = 100$

Number

Lesson 4: Adding and subtracting 10 and multiples of 10

- Add and subtract multiples of 10 to and from numbers up to 1000

Discover

Counting in 10s can help with addition and subtraction.

Learn

3-digit numbers are made up of hundreds, tens and ones.

When you add multiples of 10, the tens digit changes. The ones digit stays the same.

Example

Add: 519 + 40 = 559

Sometimes the hundreds digit will change too.

Add: 681 + 20 = 701

Lesson 5: **Adding 100 and multiples of 100**

Key words
- multiple of 100
- add

Number

- Add multiples of 100 to numbers up to 1000

Discover

Adding hundreds leaves the tens and ones unchanged.

$$2\ 8\ 7 + 300 = 587$$

Learn

As 3-digit numbers are made up of hundreds, tens and ones, when multiples of 100 are added, it is the hundreds digit that changes.

The tens and ones digits stay the same.

Example

$657 + 300 = 957$

$214 + 500 = 714$

$$6\ 5\ 7 + 300 = 957$$

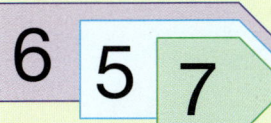

$$2\ 1\ 4 + 500 = 714$$

Lesson 6: Adding three or more small numbers

- Add three or more small numbers together

Discover

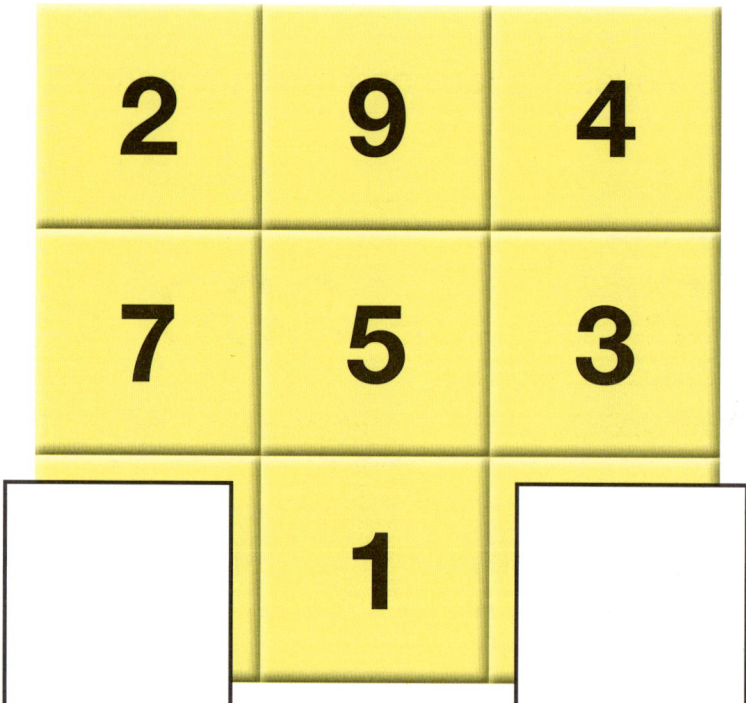

Learn

You can use different strategies to add three or more small numbers.

For example, you can look for pairs that make 10, look for helpful combinations of numbers, and start with the largest number.

Example
Add 6 + 8 + 4.
6 and 4 make 10 and 10 + 8 = 18
Add 5 + 2 + 12.
5 + 2 makes 7 and 12 + 7 = 19

Number

Lesson 7: **Using the = sign to represent equality**

Key words
• **equal to**
• **equivalent**

• Understand what the = sign means
• Use the = sign to represent equality

Discover

The numbers or number sentences on each side of the **equals** (=) symbol must balance.

$$7 + 5 \qquad = \qquad ?$$

Learn

Do you remember the **more than** and **less than** symbols (> and <)? Each is made up of two lines, with the open end pointing towards the larger number.

The equals symbol is also made of two lines, but for the equals symbol, they are the same distance apart (=). This shows whatever is on one side is **the same as** what is on the other side.

Example

$9 - 4 = 5$
$9 - 4 = 7 - 2$
$9 - 4 = 3 + 1 + 1$

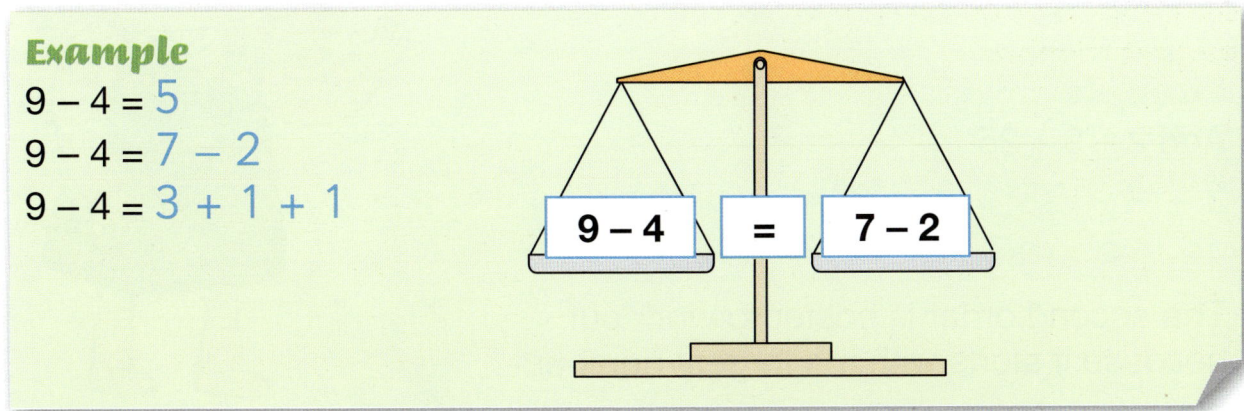

Lesson 8: **Addition in any order**

• Change the order of an addition to solve it

Key words
• addition
• order
• partition

Discover

These colours in strips are in different orders, but they all make the same total.

25	13

13	25

Learn

The order in which you add numbers does not matter. They will always have the same total.

This is helpful because it means that you can choose the order you add them to make it easier.

Example
Add 2 + 9 + 25
2 + 9 + 25 = 36
25 + 9 + 2 = 36
The second order is easier to work out because it starts with the largest number.

Lesson 1: **Totals of multiples of 5 and 100 (1)**

Key words
• multiple
• total

- Recognise multiples of 5 with a total of 100 and multiples of 100 with a total of 1000

Discover

There are many different ways of making 100 with multiples of 5.

1	2	3	4	5	6	7	8	9	10
11	12	13	14	15	16	17	18	19	20
21	22	23	24	25	26	27	28	29	30
31	32	33	34	35	36	37	38	39	40
41	42	43	44	45	46	47	48	49	50
51	52	53	54	55	56	57	58	59	60
61	62	63	64	65	66	67	68	69	70
71	72	73	74	75	76	77	78	79	80
81	82	83	84	85	86	87	88	89	90
91	92	93	94	95	96	97	98	99	100

Learn

It is very useful to know number facts and be able to recall them quickly.

If you know pairs of numbers that make 10, you can use them to help find pairs of numbers that make 100 and 1000.

Example
If you know 4 + 6 = 10, what else do you know?

400 + 600 = 1000
40 + 60 = 100
45 + 55 = 100
50 + 50 = 100

Number

Lesson 2: **Adding pairs of 2-digit numbers (1)**

• Add a pair of 2-digit numbers

Discover

You can add 2-digit numbers using a number line and partitioning.

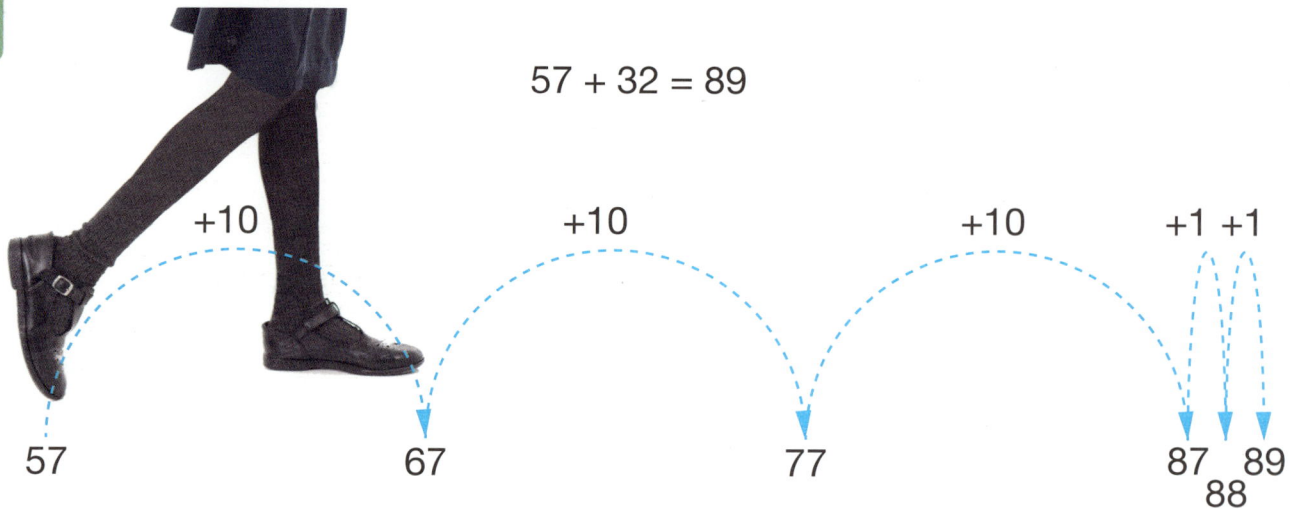

$$57 + 32 = 89$$

+10   +10   +10   +1 +1

57   67   77   87   89
                                  88

Learn

2-digit numbers can be split into parts. For example, 49 is 40 + 9.

Partitioning a number like this is helpful when you are adding pairs of 2-digit numbers. First you can count in 10s and then in 1s.

Example
Add 35 + 49

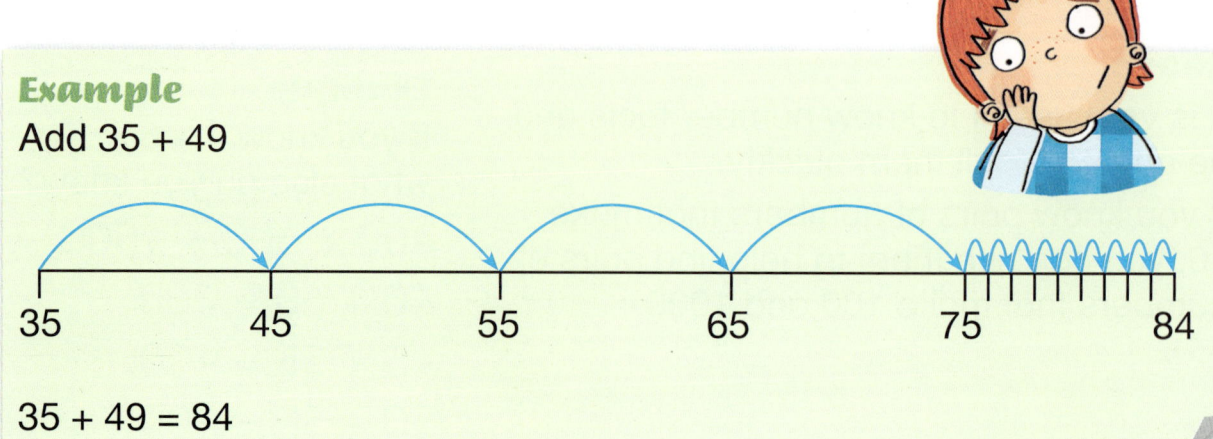

35   45   55   65   75   84

$$35 + 49 = 84$$

Lesson 3: **Subtracting pairs of 2-digit numbers (1)**

Key words
- tens
- units
- subtraction
- partition

- Subtract a pair of 2-digit numbers

Discover

You can subtract one 2-digit number from another using number lines and partitioning.

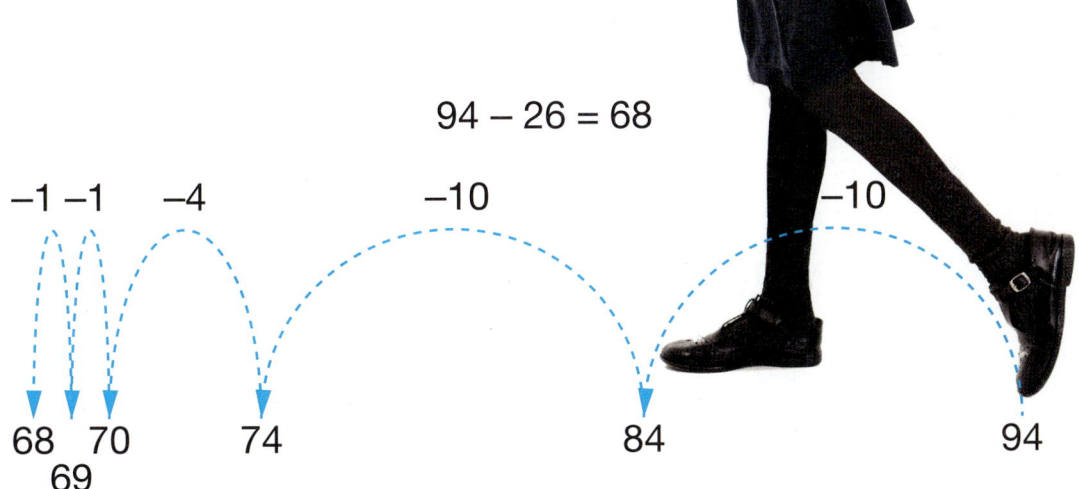

$94 - 26 = 68$

-1 -1 -4 -10 -10

68 70 74 84 94
69

Learn

To subtract a pair of 2-digit numbers, you can start with the larger number and subtract the smaller number from it.

Instead of subtracting a 2-digit number all in one go, it is helpful to split it up (partition it). So 27 becomes 20 and 7.

Example
Subtract 52 – 27

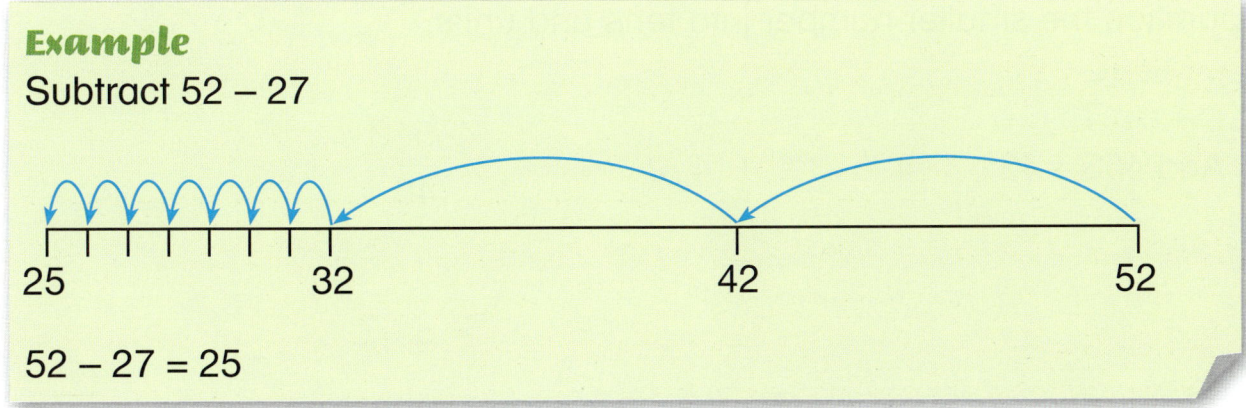

25   32   42   52

$52 - 27 = 25$

Lesson 4: **Adding 3-digit and 2-digit numbers (1)**

Number

- Add 3-digit and 2-digit numbers together

Discover

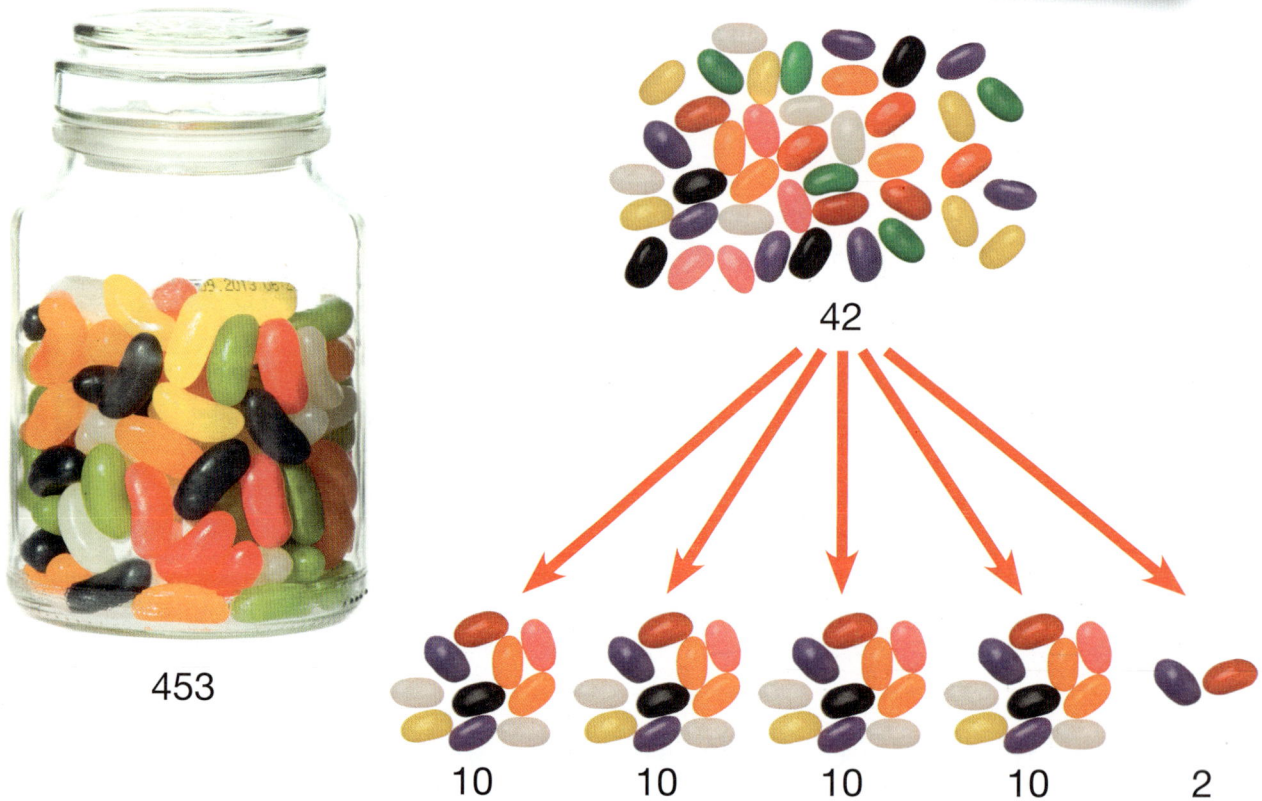

453

42

10   10   10   10   2

Learn

One way to add a 2-digit number to a 3-digit number is to partition the smaller number into tens and units.

Example

Add 453 + 42

4 5 3 + 4 2

4 5 3
40
2

4 9 5

Lesson 5: **Adding a single-digit number to a 3-digit number**

- Add single-digit numbers to 3-digit numbers

Number

Discover

When you add a small number to a large number, sometimes the tens and hundreds digits change.

add 7

Learn

Single-digit numbers such as 7 or 4 are made up of units and the digits are in the units place.

When a single-digit number is added to a 3-digit number, the digit in the units place always changes.

Sometimes the tens (and even the hundreds) place will change too.

Example

$482 + 5 = 487$ $627 + 4 = 631$ $395 + 7 = 402$

Number

Lesson 6: **Subtracting a single-digit number from a 3-digit number**

- Subtract single-digit numbers from 3-digit numbers

Discover

To subtract, you can count back.

Learn

There are several ways to subtract a single-digit number from a 3-digit number.

Sometimes the calculation can be done quickly in your head:

$287 - 1 = 286$

Sometimes the calculation crosses over a tens boundary and then a number line can be useful.

Example

$529 - 3 = 526$

$422 - 5 = 417$

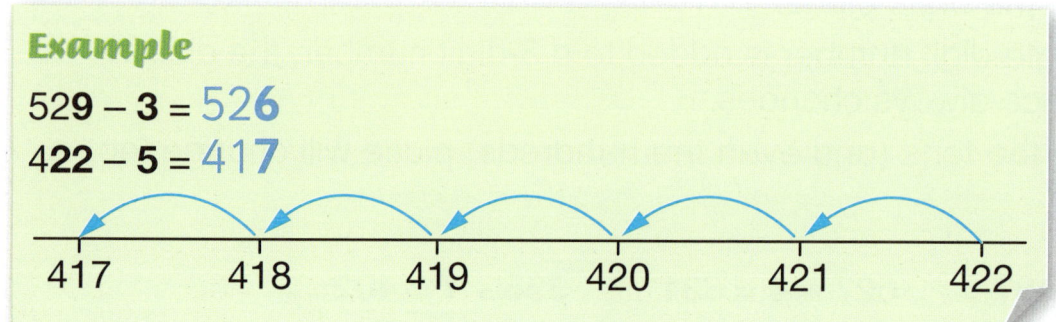

Lesson 7: **Adding multiples of 10 and 100 to 3-digit numbers**

• Find 20, 30, … 90, 100, 200, 300 more than 3-digit numbers

Discover

Adding multiples of 10 or 100 does not change the units digit.

Learn

When multiples of 10 or 100 are added to a number, the units digit stays the same. It is just the tens or hundreds digits that change.

To find a multiple of 10 or 100 more than a number, it can be helpful to step-count on in tens or hundreds.

Example

$634 + 20 = 654$ $473 + 200 = 673$ $381 + 70 = 451$

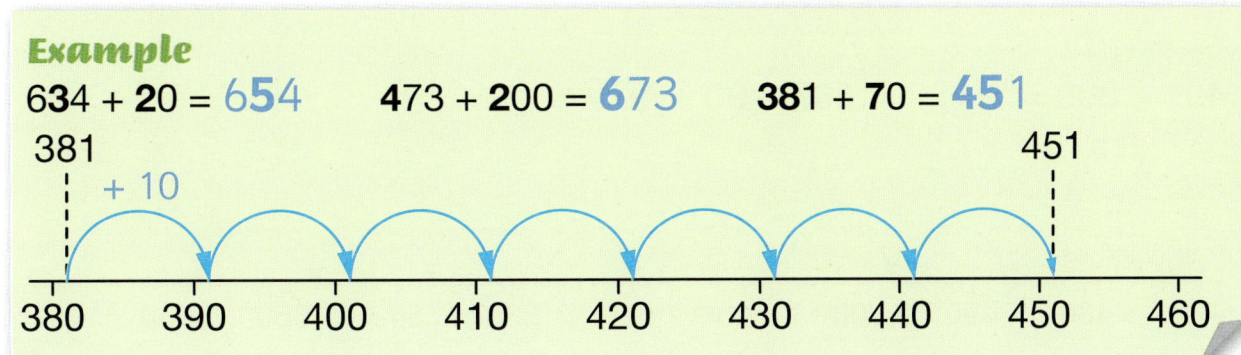

Number

Lesson 8: **Subtracting multiples of 10 and 100 from 3-digit numbers**

- Find 20, 30, … 90, 100, 200, 300 less than 3-digit numbers

Key words
- hundreds
- tens
- units
- less than

Discover

Subtracting multiples of 10 or 100 does not change the units digit.

$200 $20

$300

$40 $50

Learn

When multiples of 10 or 100 are subtracted from a number, the units digit stays the same. It is just the tens or hundreds digits that change.

To find a multiple of 10 or 100 less than a number, it may be helpful to step-count back in 10s or 100s.

Example

491 − 300 = 191   567 − 90 = 477

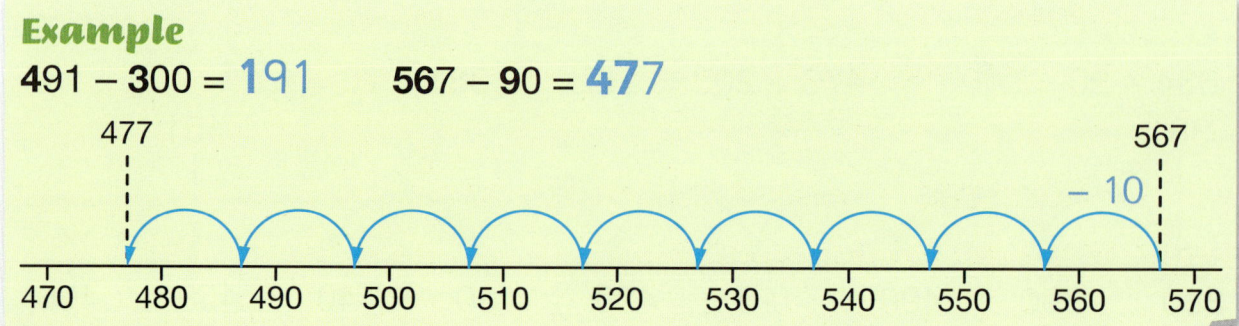

Lesson 1: **Totals of multiples of 5 and 100 (2)**

Key words
• multiple
• total

- Recall multiples of 5 with a total of 100 and multiples of 100 with a total of 1000

Discover

Multiples of 5 can be put together to make 100 in different ways.

Learn

Recalling a number fact is different from working the answer out. It means that you are able to say the answer straight away because you **know** it.

If you know an addition fact, you can work backwards to help remember subtraction facts, too. A subtraction is just an addition reversed.

Example

75 + 25 = **100**

Write down two subtraction facts.

100 − 75 = 25 and **100** − 25 = 75

400 + 600 = **1000**

Write down two subtraction facts.

1000 − 400 = 600 and **1000** − 600 = 400

Number

Lesson 2: **Finding the unknown number (1)**

- Find missing numbers in addition statements up to 100

Discover

There are many answers to these additions.

Learn

The missing number and the equals sign in a calculation can appear in different places.

$6 + ? = 20$

$? + 3 = 15$

$14 = 8 + ?$

Wherever the missing number is in a calculation, the other numbers can be used to solve the problem.

Example

Fill in the missing numbers.

$6 + ? = 20$ $20 - 6 = 14$, so $6 + \textbf{14} = 20$

$? + 3 = 15$ $15 - 3 = \textbf{12}$, so $\textbf{12} + 3 = 15$

$14 = 8 + ?$ $14 - 8 = \textbf{5}$, so $14 = 8 + \textbf{5}$

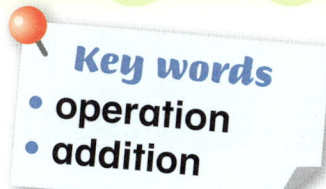

Lesson 3: **Finding the unknown number (2)**

Key words
- operation
- addition

- Find missing numbers in addition statements up to 100

Discover

If you know an addition, you also know two subtractions.

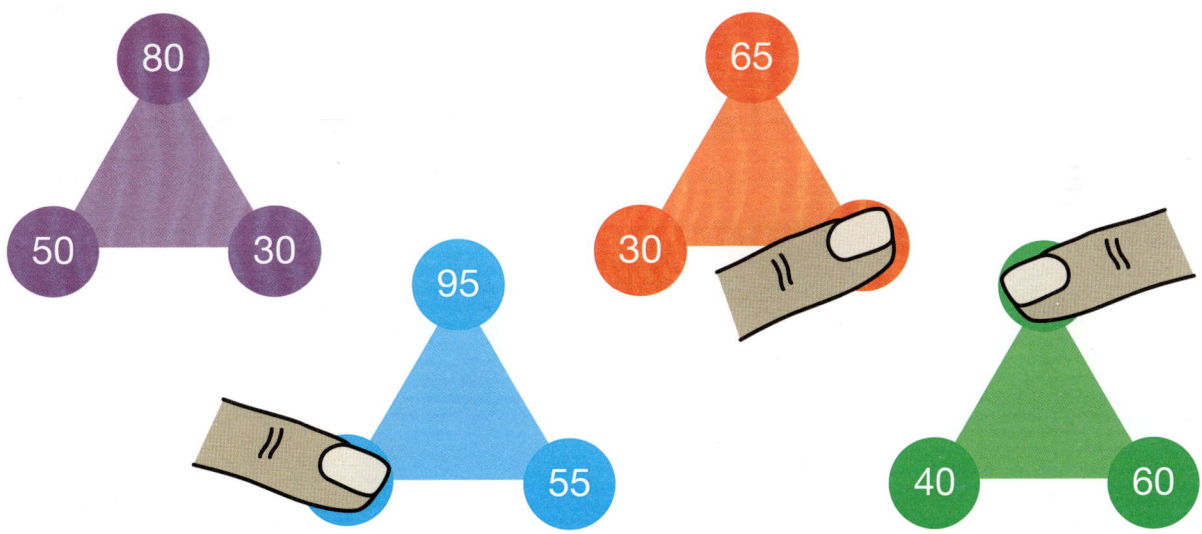

Learn

Addition and subtraction number facts are linked. As well as writing $78 + 22 = 100$, you can write $22 + 78 = 100$, $100 - 22 = 78$ and $100 - 78 = 22$.

So when there is an unknown number in a calculation, you can use the numbers you already know to help.

Example

Find the missing number.

$43 + ? = 100$

$100 - 43 = 57$, so the missing number is 57.

$50 = ? - 24$

$50 + 24 = 74$, so the missing number is 74.

Lesson 4: **Adding pairs of 2-digit numbers (2)**

- Add a pair of 2-digit numbers

Key words
- digit
- hundreds
- tens
- units
- partition

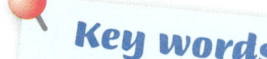

Discover

Splitting numbers into tens and ones makes it easier to add them.

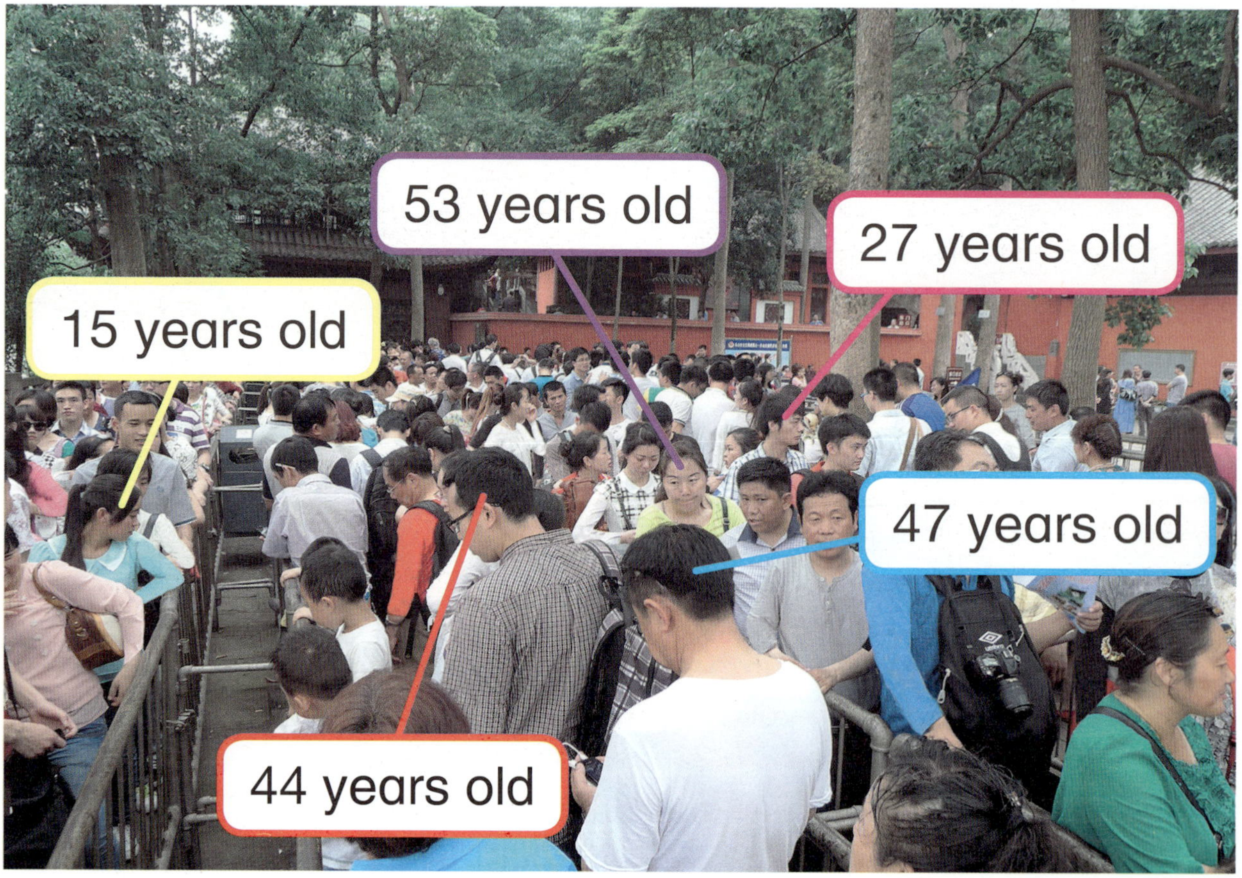
53 years old
27 years old
15 years old
47 years old
44 years old

Learn

Every 2-digit number is a combination of tens and units. When you are adding a pair of 2-digit numbers, it can help to partition at least one of the numbers into tens and units.

Example

Work out 44 + 27.

$44 + 27 = 44 + 20 + 7$
$= 64 + 7$
$= 71$

So $44 + 27 = 71$

Lesson 5: **Subtracting pairs of 2-digit numbers (2)**

• Subtract a pair of 2-digit numbers

Key words
• digit
• difference
• hundreds
• tens
• units
• partition

Discover

There is more than one way to subtract.

Green team: 18 fans

Blue team: 42 fans

Red team: 23 fans

Yellow team: 69 fans

Learn

Instead of subtracting a 2-digit number from another 2-digit number all in one go, it is useful to split the second number up into tens and units.

If the numbers are close together, you can also count up from the smaller number to the larger to find the difference.

Example

$$69 - 23 = 69 - 20 - 3$$
$$= 49 - 3$$
$$= 49$$
$$\text{So } 69 - 23 = 46$$

Number

Lesson 6: **Adding 3-digit and 2-digit numbers (2)**

• Add 3-digit and 2-digit numbers together

Discover

The counting machine has hundreds, tens and units buttons underneath.

To add a 2-digit number, you press the buttons, once for every ten and unit.

Learn

When a 2-digit number is added to a 3-digit number, the tens and units in the larger number change.

To be able to do this, we need to first partition the 2-digit number into its tens and its units. Then, we can add each separately.

Example

On the counting machine, press the tens button 4 times and the units button 7 times.

$$238 + 47 = 238 + 40 + 7$$
$$= 278 + 7$$
$$= 285$$

Lesson 7: **Adding and subtracting a single-digit number to and from a 3-digit number**

- Add and subtract single-digit numbers to and from 3-digit numbers

Key words
- units
- more than
- less than
- tens boundary
- hundreds boundary

Discover

Finding a single digit more or less than a number is often something you can do in your head.

Learn

It is quicker to use number bonds or patterns that you know already than to count on every time.

Sometimes the tens and hundreds digits will change, as well as the units digit.

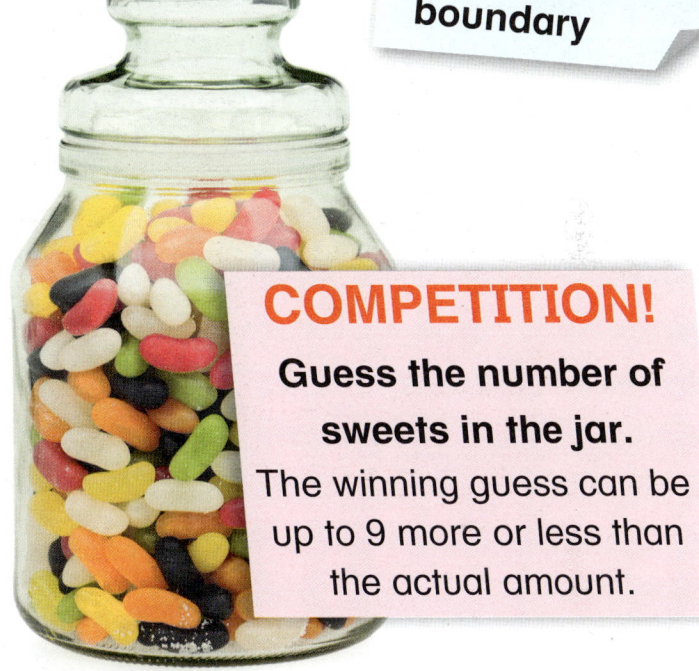

COMPETITION!

Guess the number of sweets in the jar.

The winning guess can be up to 9 more or less than the actual amount.

Example

723 + 1 = 724   536 − 2 = 534
789 + 3 = 792   531 − 7 = 524
796 + 5 = 801   503 − 5 = 498

Number

Lesson 8: **Adding and subtracting multiples of 10 and 100 to and from 3-digit numbers**

- Find 20, 30, … 90, 100, 200, 300 more and less than 3-digit numbers

Discover

Taking money out of a cash machine (ATM) is a bit like doing a subtraction of multiples of 10.

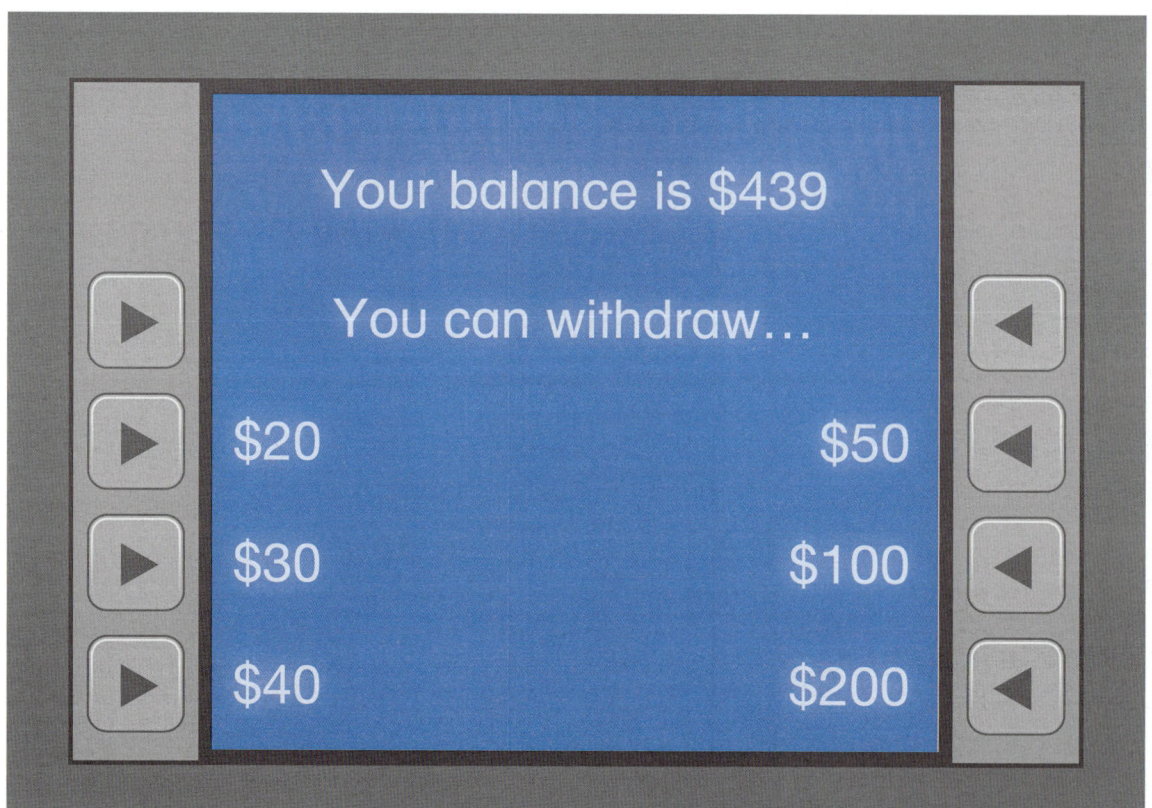

Your balance is $439

You can withdraw…

$20 $50

$30 $100

$40 $200

Learn

Multiples of 10 and 100 both have a zero in the units place. So, when they are added to or subtracted from a 3-digit number, the units of that number stay the same.

Example
$532 + 20 = 552$
$833 - 50 = 783$
$756 - 300 = 456$
$457 + 200 = 657$

Lesson 1: Multiplication and division facts for 2×, 3×, 5× and 10× tables (1)

Number

- Recall multiplication and division facts for the 2×, 3×, 5× and 10× tables

Discover

Using a multiplication grid is a helpful way to learn multiplication tables.

×	2	3	4	5	6	7	8	9	10	11	12
2									●		
3						●					
5		●									
10	●										

Learn

Multiplication and division are the opposite or **inverse** of each other. Times-tables facts can be used to answer both multiplication and division calculations.

Example

Write a division for each multiplication.

$4 \times 10 = 40$ $40 \div 10 = 4$

$3 \times 5 = 15$ $15 \div 5 = 3$

$9 \times 2 = 18$ $18 \div 2 = 9$

Number

Lesson 2: **Multiplication and division facts for 2×, 3×, 5× and 10× tables (2)**

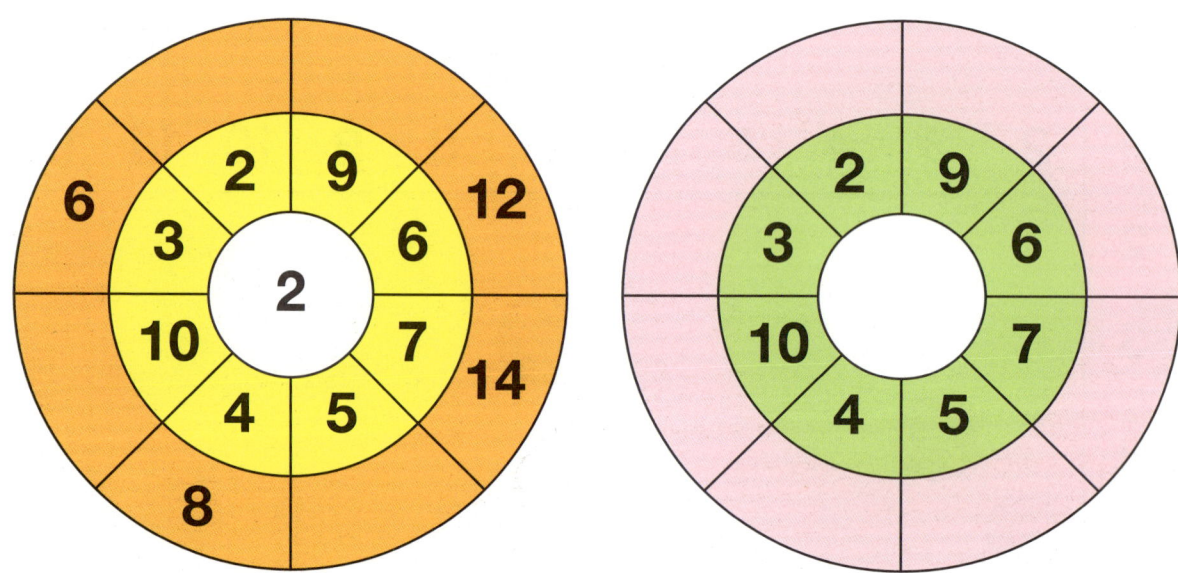

Key words
- multiply
- times
- times table
- divide
- multiple

- Recall multiplication and division facts for the 2×, 3×, 5× and 10× tables

Discover

Knowing the times tables helps with division.

Learn

Knowing multiplication and division facts is an important maths skill. Learning these facts so that you can recall them quickly takes time. It is important to keep practising.

A good way to memorise times-table facts is to skip-count through the multiples.

Example
What is 7 × 5?

5, 10, 15, 20, 25, 30, **35**
So, 7 × 5 = **35**

Lesson 3: **Multiplication and division facts for the 4× table (1)**

Key words
• multiply
• times
• times tables
• divide
• multiple

• Recall the 4× tables facts

Discover

Every other even number is a multiple of 4.

1 car = 4 tyres
2 cars = ?
3 cars = ?

Learn

It is better to learn and remember times-tables facts, rather than having to work each one out. The way to do this is to look for patterns and to practise them regularly.

Just like the mechanic in the picture, if you can count in 4s, you can answer 4× table questions.

Example

What is 5×4?

4, 8, 12, 16, **20**

So, $5 \times 4 = $ **20**

What is $32 \div 4$?

4, 8, 12, 16, 20, 24, 28, **32**

This is eight fours, so, $32 \div 4 = $ **8**

Lesson 4: **Multiplication and division facts for the 4× table (2)**

- Recall the 4× tables facts

Discover

If you know the 2× table facts, you you can use these to help work out the 4× table facts.

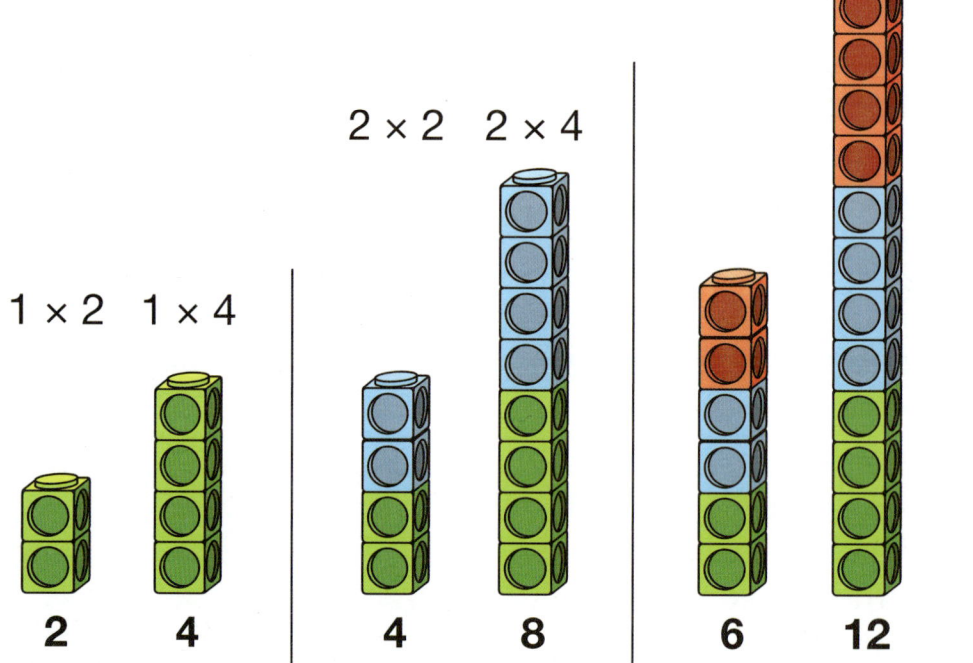

Learn

To work out the answers to the 4 multiplication facts, double the answers to the 2 multiplication facts.

Example

Complete the multiplications.

1 × 2 = 2	1 × 4 = 4
2 × 2 = 4	2 × 4 = 8
3 × 2 = 6	3 × 4 = 12
4 × 2 = 8	4 × 4 = 16

Lesson 5: **Multiples of 2, 5 and 10**

Key words
- multiple
- even
- units
- digit

- Recognise 2- and 3-digit multiples of 2, 5 and 10.

Number

Discover

A **multiple** is a number in a particular times table.

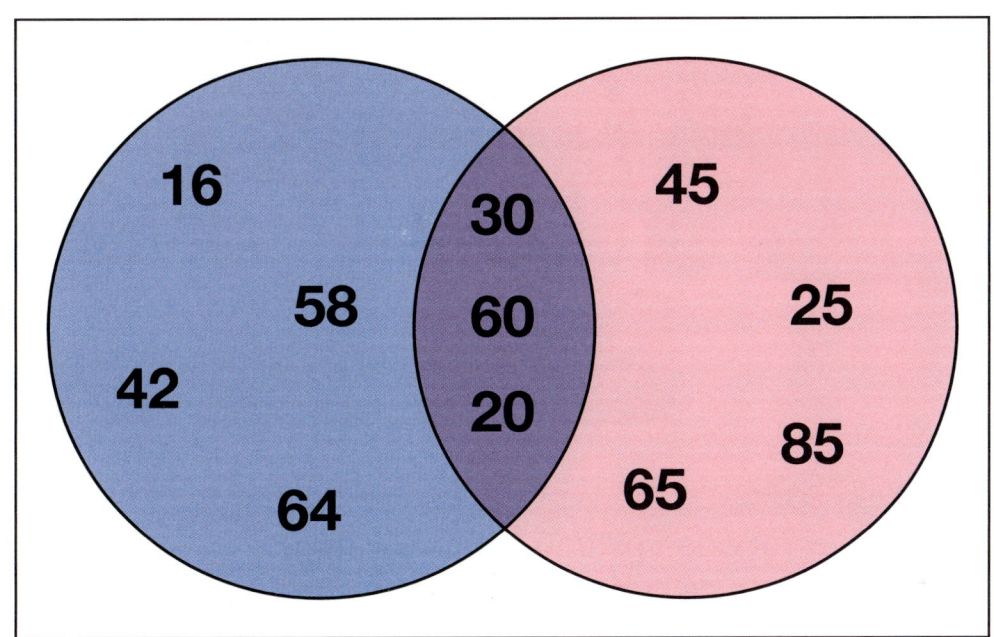

Learn

All even numbers are multiples of 2.

Multiples of 5 always end in 5 or 0.

Multiples of 10 always end in 0.

Example

Is the number 45 a multiple of 2, 5 or 10?

45 is not a multiple of 2 because it is not even and not in the 2× table.

45 is a multiple of 5 because 9 × 5 = 45.

45 is not a multiple of 10 because it does not end in a 0 and is not in the 10× table.

Number

Lesson 6: **Halving and doubling (1)**

- Understand the links between halving and doubling numbers

Discover

Halving and **doubling** are the opposite or **inverse** of each other.

Learn

Halving a number means splitting it into two equal parts. This is the same as dividing by 2.

Doubling a number means making it worth twice as much. This is the same as multiplying by 2.

If a number is halved, it can be doubled to get back to the original number.

Example

What is half of 12?

Half of 12 is 6.

What is double 6?

Double 6 is 12.

58

Lesson 7: **Multiplying 2-digit numbers by 10**

- Multiply 2-digit numbers by 10

Key words
- multiply
- multiple of 10
- units
- digits

Discover

Instead of **repeated addition**, it is quicker to use **multiplication**.

My Savings

Week 1 ✓

Week 2 ✓

Week 3 ✓

Week 4 ✓

Week 5 ✓

Week 6 ✓

Week 7 ✓

Week 8 ✓

Week 9 ✓

Week 10 ✓

Learn

Instead of adding the same number 10 times, it is quicker to multiply it by 10.

When you multiply a 2-digit number by 10, the digits shift one place to the left because they are then each worth 10 times as much. The units column is then empty so you use a zero to show this.

Example

If you save $45 a week, how much will you have in 10 weeks? $45 \times 10 = 450$

H	T	U
	4	5
4	5	0

$45 \times 10 = 450$

If you save $45 a week, you will have a total of $450 in 10 weeks.

Number

Lesson 8: **Multiplication in any order**

- Multiply numbers in any order and understand the answer will be the same

Discover

Multiplications can be written in different ways.

Learn

If you multiply two numbers together, it doesn't matter which order they are in. They always give the same answer.

Example
Show two ways of multiplying 2 and 5.

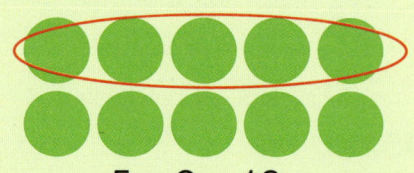

$$5 \times 2 = 10$$

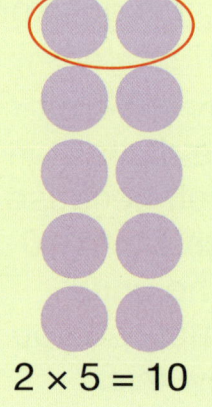

$$2 \times 5 = 10$$

Lesson 1: **Multiplication and division facts for 2×, 3×, 4×, 5× and 10× tables (1)**

- Recall multiplication and division facts for the 2×, 3×, 4×, 5× and 10× tables

Key words
- **multiply**
- **times**
- **divide**
- **multiple**
- **digit**

Discover

Multiplication facts can be used to help recall division facts as they are linked.

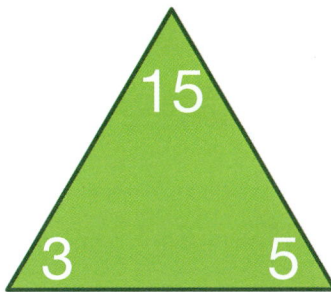

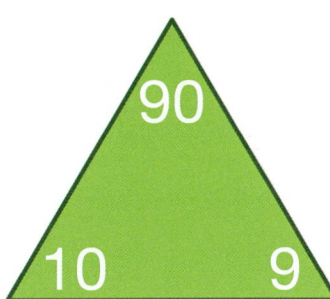

Learn

It is important to be able to recall multiplication and division facts quickly. The best way to become better at this is through practice.

Multiplication facts help you remember division facts.

Example

Write a division for each multiplication.

8 × 4 = 32 helps you remember
32 ÷ 4 = 8.

9 × 3 = 27 helps you remember
27 ÷ 3 = 9.

Number

Lesson 2: **Doubles of numbers to 20 and related halves**

- Double numbers up to 20 and find half of the answers

Discover

Halving is the inverse of doubling.

Learn

Doubling means making something twice as large:

$10 \times 2 = 20$ so double 10 is 20.

Halving means sharing a number into two equal parts:

$16 \div 2 = 8$ so half of 16 is 8.

Example

Double 15.

30 because $15 + 15 = 30$

Find half of 20.

10 because $20 \div 2 = 10$

Lesson 3: **Doubles of multiples of 5 and related halves**

Key words
• double
• twice
• halve/half
• multiple

Number

• Double multiples of 5 and find half of the answer

Discover

How could you work out the missing numbers?

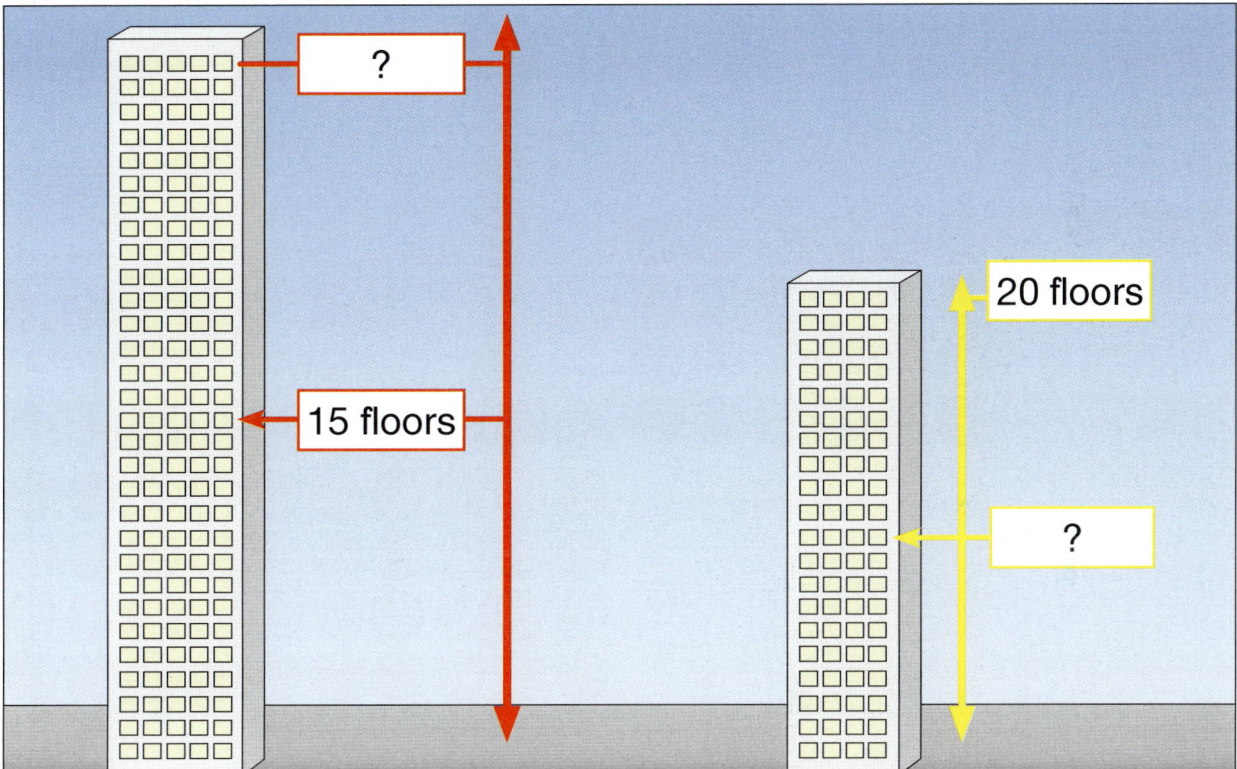

?

15 floors

20 floors

?

Learn

Doubling a number and halving the answer gives you the starting number.

A quick way to double 2-digit numbers is to double the tens, double the units and then add them together.

Example
Double 25 and double 65

Double 25 = Double 20 + Double 5
　　　　　= 40 + 10
　　　　　= 50
Double 65 = Double 60 + Double 5
　　　　　= 120 + 10
　　　　　= 130

Number

Lesson 4: **Multiplying single-digit numbers by 2, 3, 4, 5, 6, 9 and 10 (1)**

- Multiply a single-digit number by 2, 3, 4, 5, 6, 9 or 10

Discover

Arrays can show multiplications.

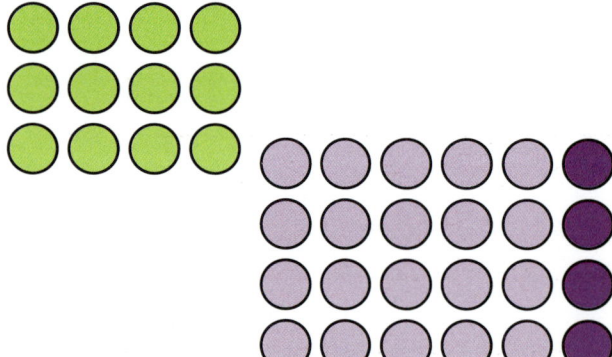

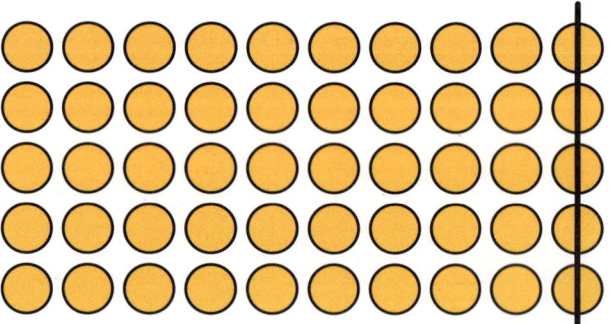

Learn

If you know the 5× and 10× tables, you can use these to help with the 6× and 9× tables.

To multiply a number by 6, multiply it by 5 then add on **another one of that number**.

To multiply a number by 9, multiply it by 10 then **subtract one of that number**.

Example

Work out 8×6.

$8 \times 6 = 8 \times 5 + 8$

$ = 40 + 8$

$ = 48$

Work out 6×9.

$6 \times 9 = 6 \times 10 - 6$

$ = 60 - 6$

$ = 54$

Lesson 5: **Multiplying single-digit numbers by 2, 3, 4, 5, 6, 9 and 10 (2)**

- Multiply a single-digit number by 2, 3, 4, 5, 6, 9 or 10

Key words
- array
- multiply
- times
- multiple
- product

Number

Discover

Counting in multiples is similar to skip-counting and it can help to work out multiplication facts.

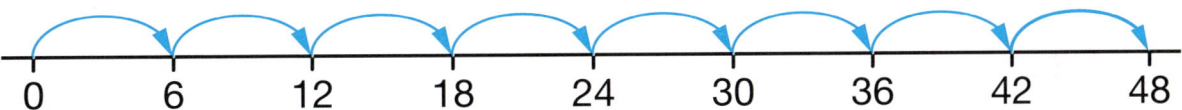

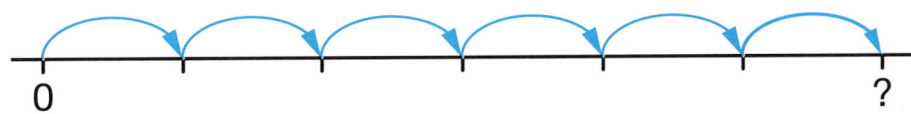

Learn

One way to practise multiplication facts is to count through multiples until you get to the answer. As you keep saying the multiples, it helps you remember them.

Example
What are seven 9s?
9, 18, 27, 36, 45, 54, 63
So $7 \times 9 = 63$
What is the product of 3 and 6?
6, 12, 18
So $3 \times 6 = 18$

Number

Lesson 6: **Dividing 2-digit numbers by 2, 3, 4, 5, 6, 9 and 10 (1)**

- Divide a 2-digit number by 2, 3, 4, 5, 6, 9 or 10

Discover

Some numbers can be divided into equal groups in more than one way.

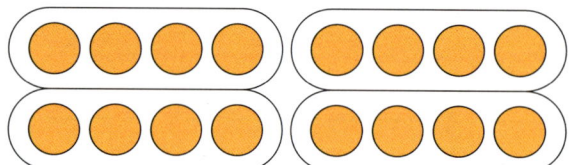 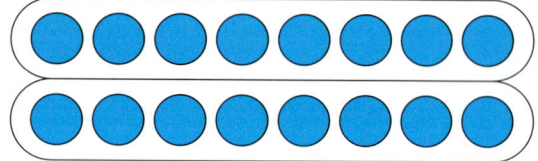

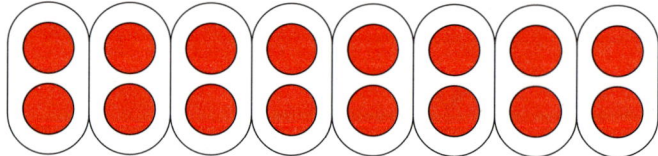

Learn

Division means sharing a larger number into smaller groups of equal size. The number of groups that fit into the number is the answer.

Example
Share 42 between 7.

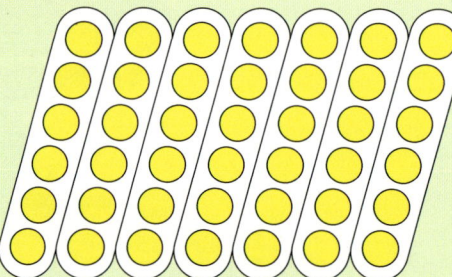

42 counters can be shared into 7 groups of 6, so $42 \div 7 = 6$.

Lesson 7: **Dividing 2-digit numbers by 2, 3, 4, 5, 6, 9 and 10 (2)**

- Divide a 2-digit number by 2, 3, 4, 5, 6, 9 and 10

> **Key words**
> - divide
> - split
> - share
> - multiple
> - remainder

Discover

Division is like subtracting lots of times.

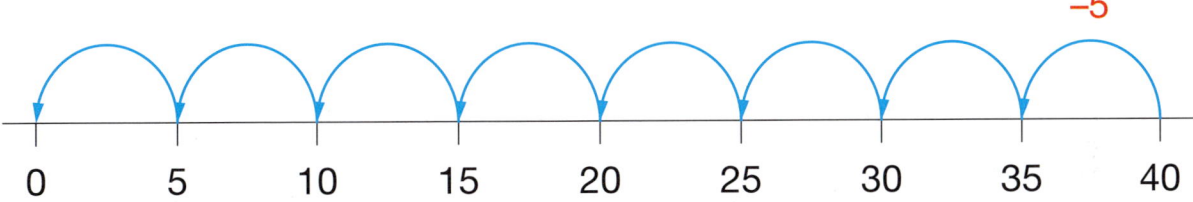

You can also use counting on to find answers to division questions. To find 37 divided by 4 it is easier to count on.

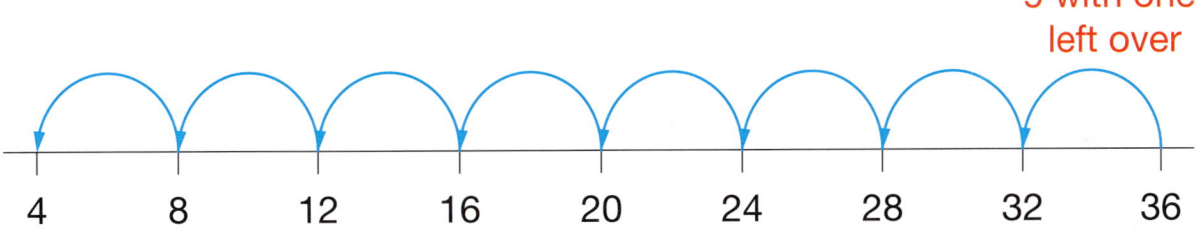

Learn

One way to practise division facts is to subtract the smaller number again and again from the larger number to see how many times it fits into it.

Sometimes a number will not divide exactly. The amount left over is called the **remainder**.

> **Example**
> What is $60 \div 10$?
>
> 60, 50, 40, 30, 20, 10, 0 is six jumps of 10
> So $60 \div 10 = 6$

Lesson 8: **Linking multiplication and division**

Number

- Understand how multiplication and division are linked
- Write related multiplication and division facts

Discover

A

There are 6 tables of 4 children in our class. That's a multiplication fact. 6 groups of 4 children equals 24 children altogether.

B

No it's not. It's a division fact. 24 children in the class split into 6 groups equals 4 in each group.

C

You're both right. It depends on how you look at it.

Learn

You can use multiplication facts to help answer division questions (and the other way around).

Example

$72 \div 9 = \boxed{}$

I know that there are eight 9s in 72 because $8 \times 9 = 72$, so the answer is 8.

$4 \times 5 = \boxed{}$

I know that there are four 5s in 20 because $20 \div 5 = 4$, so the answer is 20.

Lesson 1: **Multiplication and division facts for 2×, 3×, 4×, 5× and 10× tables (2)**

- Recall multiplication and division facts for the 2×, 3×, 4×, 5× and 10× tables

Key words
- multiply
- times
- divide
- multiple
- digit

Discover

Multiplication is a quick way of adding lots of the same number.

Cake Sale $3 each

Learn

If you know the multiplication facts, you don't need to keep adding the same number again and again.

Multiplication facts can be used to help with division questions, too.

Example
Work out:

$2 + 2 + 2 + 2 + 2 + 2 + 2 + 2 + 2$

Using multiplication facts,
$9 \times 2 = 18$

Number

Lesson 2: Halving and doubling (2)

* Double numbers up to 20 and multiples of 5 less than 100 and halve the answers

Key words
* double
* twice
* halve/half
* multiple

Discover

A number may be double one number and half of another.

10	70	12	80
18	6	40	36
35	24	20	3

Learn

If you know how to double small numbers, you can double multiples of 5 easily by partitioning the number into tens and units.

Example
Double 65

Double 65 = Double 60 + Double 5
          = 120 + 10
          = 130

Lesson 3: **Doubling multiples of 50**

- Double multiples of 50 to 500

Key words
- double
- twice
- multiple

Number

Discover

You can use facts about doubling that you know already to help with numbers you do not know.

Regular

250 g

50 g

Double size

600 ml

Learn

If you know how to double multiples of 5, you can double multiples of 50. The answer is just 10 times more.

Example
Double 35 and double 350

Double 35 = Double 30 + Double 5
= 60 + 10
= 70

Double 350 = Double 300 + Double 50
= 600 + 100
= 700

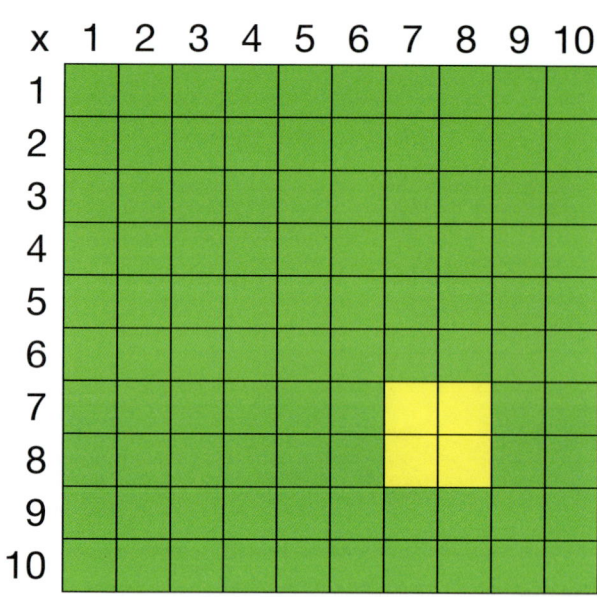

Number

Lesson 4: **Multiplying single-digit numbers by 2, 3, 4, 5, 6, 9 and 10 (3)**

- Multiply a single-digit number by 2, 3, 4, 5, 6, 9 or 10

Key words
- array
- multiply
- times
- product

Discover

Knowing the multiplication tables for 2, 3, 4, 5, 6, 9 and 10 gives you almost all of the multiplication facts to 10×10.

Learn

You can multiply single-digit numbers by 2, 3, 4, 5, 6, 9 or 10 by:

- repeated addition
- using known times tables to help
- learning the times-table fact.

Example
Multiply: 7×6

$6 \times 7 = 7 + 7 + 7 + 7 + 7 + 7$
$\qquad = 42$

$6 \times 7 = 6 \times 5$ and add two more 6s
$\qquad = 30 + 6 + 6$
$\qquad = 42$

$6 \times 6 = 36$, so $6 \times 7 = 42$

Number

Lesson 5: **Multiplying teens numbers by 3 and 5 (1)**

- Multiply a teens number by 3 and 5

Key words
- tens
- units
- multiply
- partition

Discover

How could you use arrow cards to help work out 16 × 3?

Learn

2-digit numbers can be split into their tens and units.

When multiplying a teens number by 3 and 5, the teens number can be partitioned to help work out the answer.

Example

Multiply 17 × 5

17 × 5 = 10 × 5 + 7 × 5

= 50 + 35

= 85

Lesson 6: **Multiplying teens numbers by 3 and 5 (2)**

- Multiply a teens number by 3 and 5

Discover

The 5 and 3 times tables do not just stop at 10!

Eat 5 a day

Brush 3 times a day

Learn

If you know what 10 times a number is, you can use this to help multiply using numbers that are in the teens.

Ten 3s are 30, so 14 × 3 equals 30 plus another four 3s.

Ten 5s are 50, so 16 × 5 equals 50 plus another six 5s.

Example

Work out 16 × 5

$$16 × 5 = 10 × 5 + 6 × 5$$
$$= 50 + 30$$
$$= 80$$

Lesson 7: **Dividing 2-digit numbers by 2, 3, 4, 5, 6, 9 and 10 (3)**

- Divide a 2-digit number by 2, 3, 4, 5, 6, 9 or 10

Key words
- divide
- split
- share
- multiple

Number

Discover

Dividing a number is the same as splitting it into equal groups.

Learn

You can divide 2-digit numbers by 2, 3, 4, 5, 6, 9 or 10 by:

a counting the multiples

b using a times-table fact you know to help.

Example

What is 36 ÷ 9?

a 9, 18, 27, 36 = four 9s in 36

b 4 × 9 = 36, so 36 ÷ 9 = 4

Number

Lesson 8: Dividing 2-digit numbers by 2, 3, 4, 5, 6, 9 and 10 (4)

- Divide a 2-digit number by 2, 3, 4, 5, 6, 9 or 10

Key words
- divide
- split
- share
- multiple

Discover

Counting in multiples can help you divide.

This number line shows $60 \div 4$ split into two easier calculations.

How many jumps are there altogether?

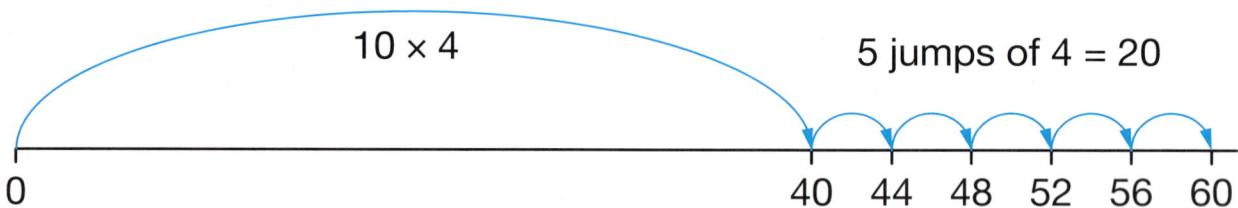

10 jumps of 4 = 40

10×4

5 jumps of 4 = 20

0   40   44   48   52   56   60

Learn

One way of dividing 2-digit numbers by 2, 3, 4, 5, 6, 9 or 10 is to count in multiples and see how many fit into the number.

Example

How many 6s are in 78?

There are ten 6s in 60.

78 is three 6s more than 60 (66, 72, 78).

So, $78 \div 6 = 10 + 3$

$\qquad = 13$

Lesson 1: **Identifying and describing 2D shapes**

- Identify, describe and draw regular and irregular 2D shapes according to their properties

Discover

You know what a shape is by the number of sides and vertices it has.

Learn

A pentagon has 5 sides and 5 vertices.
A hexagon has 6 sides and 6 vertices.
A vertex is also an angle.

Example

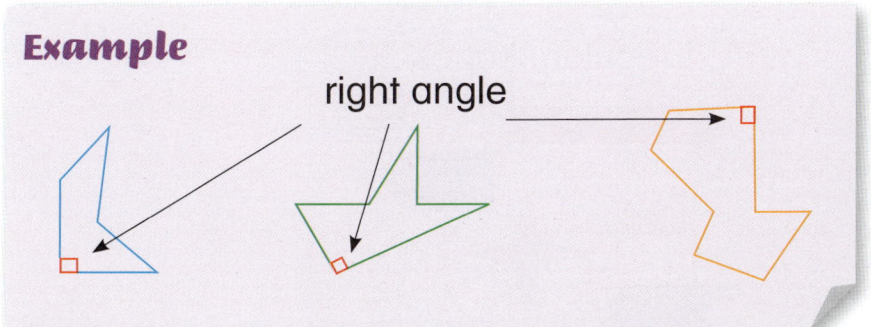

right angle

Geometry

77

Lesson 2: **Drawing 2D shapes**

• Recognise 2D shapes in drawings

Discover

You can see lots of shapes in these pictures.

Geometry

Learn

A regular shape has sides and vertices that are all equal. An irregular shape has sides and vertices that are not equal.

Example

Regular shapes   Irregular shapes

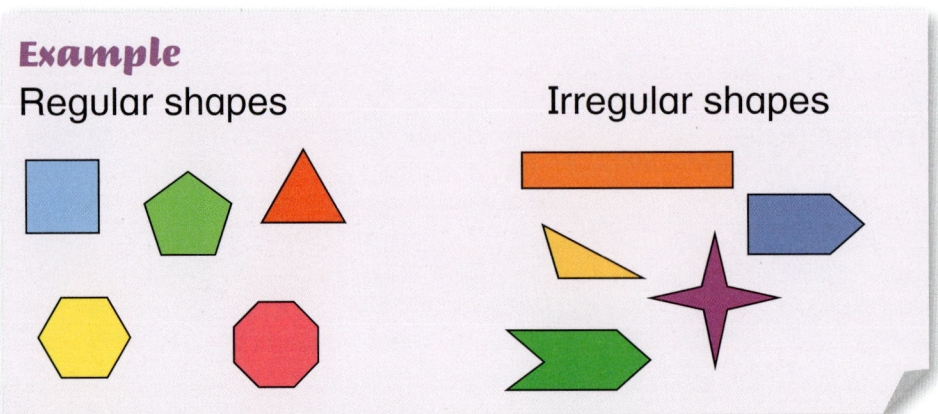

Lesson 3: **2D shapes and right angles**

- Identify 2D shapes and right angles in the environment

Key words
- quarter turn
- right angle
- degrees

Discover

We can see right angles all around us.

Learn

A right angle is a quarter of a turn, which is 90°. 2 right angles make a half turn. 3 make a three-quarter turn and 4 right angles will make a full turn.

Example

Geometry

79

Lesson 4: **2D shapes and symmetry**

- Identify symmetry in shapes and the environment

Discover

These pictures all show symmetry in nature. Can you think of other examples?

Learn

An object is symmetrical if you can divide it into identical halves that mirror each other.

Example

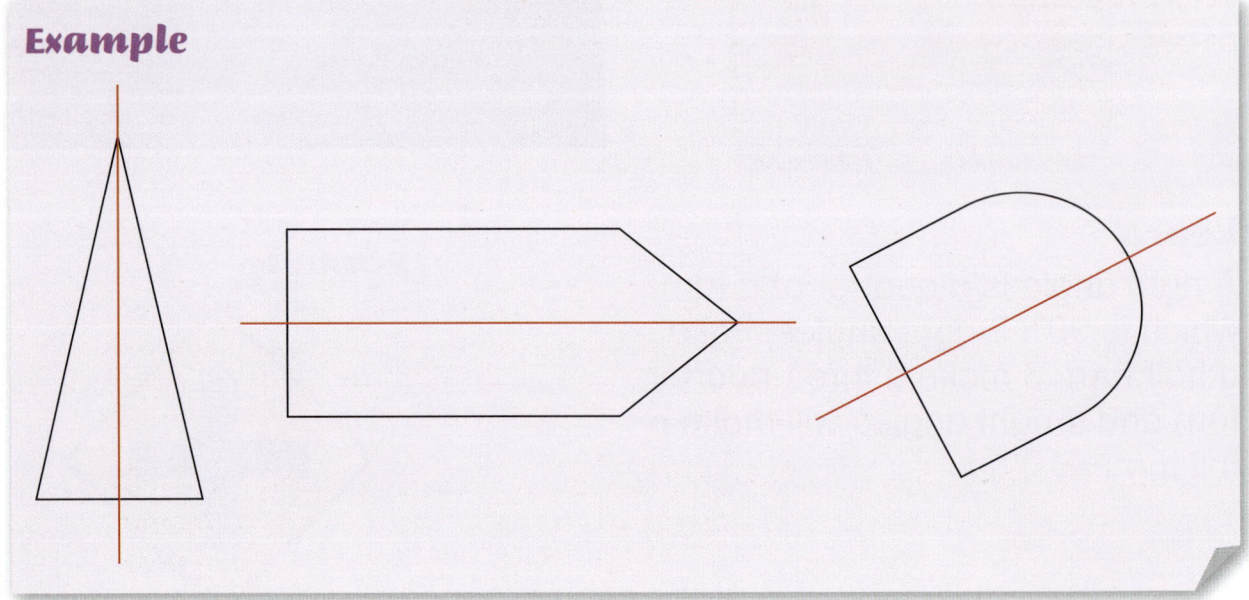

Geometry

Lesson 1: **Identifying 3D shapes**

- Identify, describe and classify 3D shapes

Discover

These pyramids are in Egypt. They have 4 triangular faces and 1 square face. They have 5 vertices and 8 edges.

Learn

The properties of 3D shapes

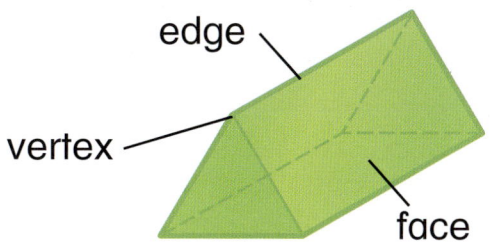

edge

vertex

face

Example

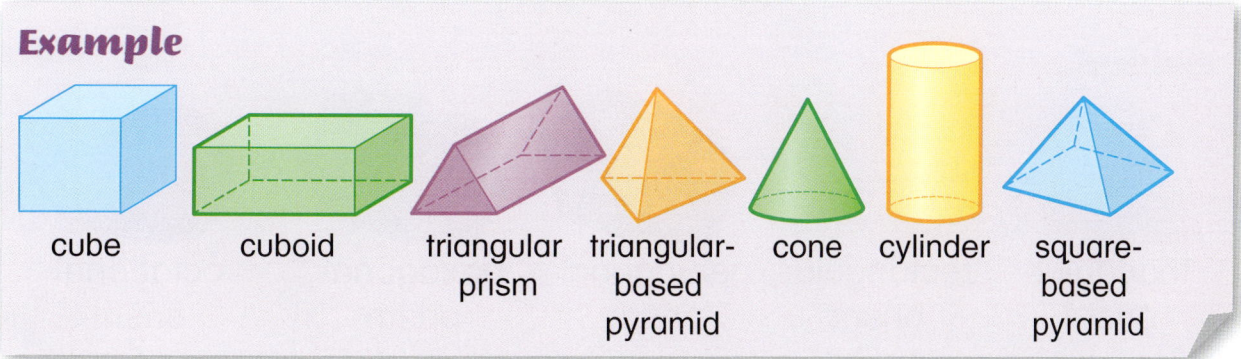

| cube | cuboid | triangular prism | triangular-based pyramid | cone | cylinder | square-based pyramid |

Geometry

81

Lesson 2: **Making 3D shapes**

- Identify the properties of a prism

Key words
- prism
- rectangular prism
- pentagonal prism
- hexagonal prism
- octagonal prism

Discover

This tent is like a triangular prism.
It has 2 triangular faces, 3 rectangular
faces, 9 edges and 6 vertices.

Learn

A prism is a 3D shape with 2 identical ends and flat sides.
The cross-section is the same all along its length.
The shape of the ends gives the prism its name.

Example

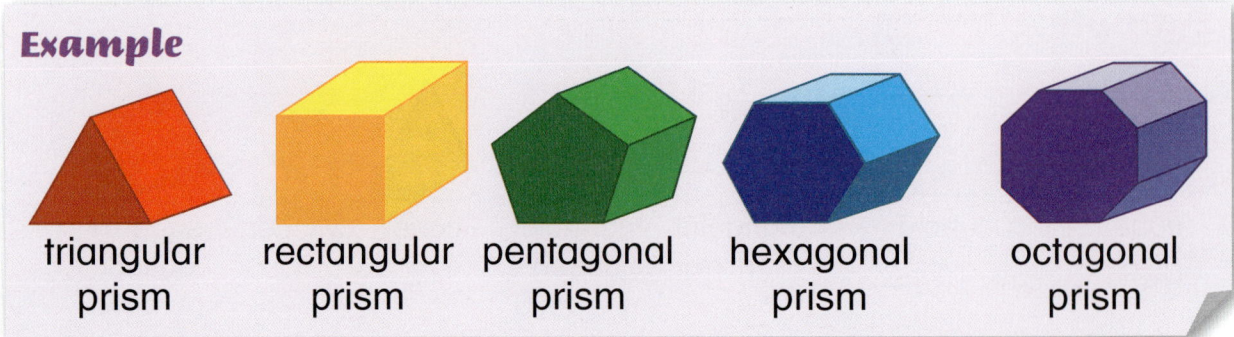

| triangular prism | rectangular prism | pentagonal prism | hexagonal prism | octagonal prism |

Geometry

Lesson 3: **Nets of a cube**

• Draw a net for a cube and make a cube

Discover

This is a cube and its net. A cube is a 3D shape with edges, vertices and flat faces.
It has 6 square faces, 8 vertices and 12 edges.

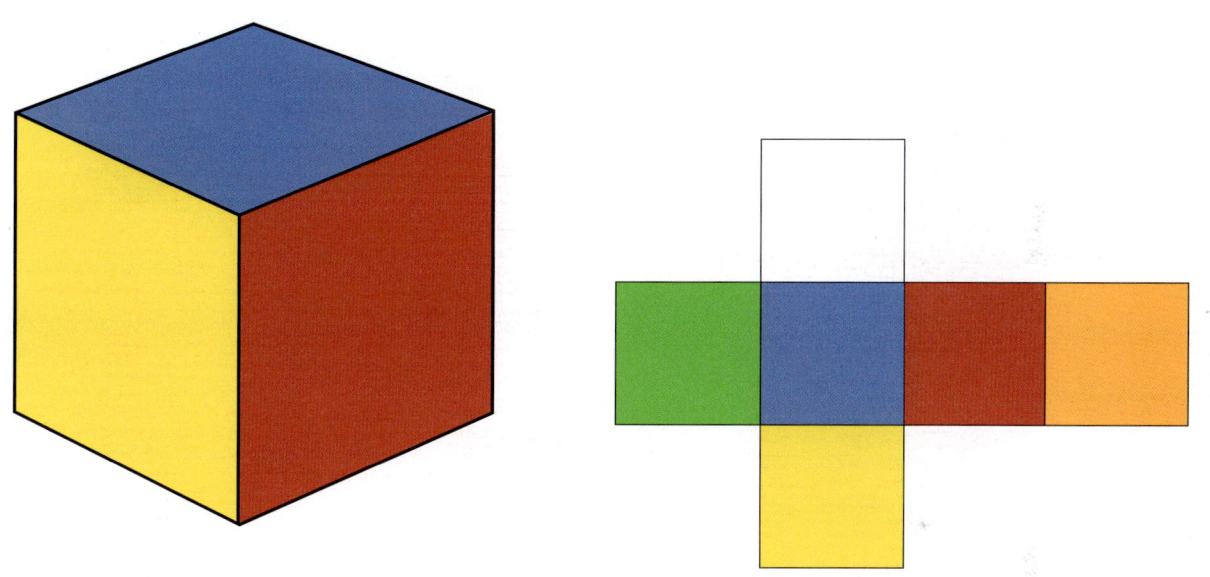

Learn

You can make a cube from a net. The net for a cube is made up of 6 squares.

Example

Geometry

Lesson 4: **Recognising 3D shapes**

- Recognise 3D shapes in drawings and in the environment

Discover

What shapes can you see here? Look around the classroom. What 3D shapes can you see?
What 3D shapes can you see in the pictures below?

Learn

Pictures often show objects made from 3D shapes.
What shapes can you see in this picture?

Geometry

Lesson 1: **Position, direction and movement (1)**

- Use the language of position and place objects in different positions

Discover

You can say where in the cupboard the objects are, using words to describe their positions. Can you describe the position of some of the objects?

Learn

You use words such as: **under**, **in front of**, **to the right of** to describe position. For example: **The cube is to the right of the sphere**.

Example

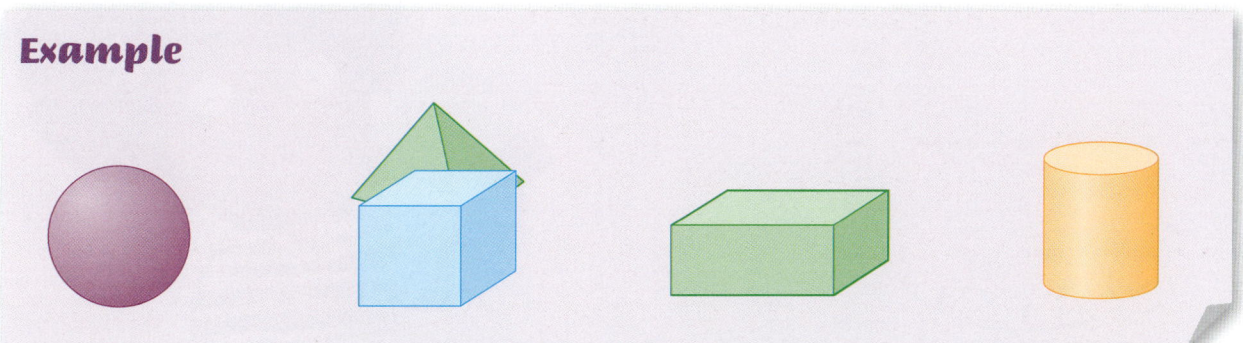

Geometry

Lesson 2: **Position, direction and movement (2)**

- Describe movement and move in different directions

Key words
- direction
- clockwise
- anticlockwise
- right
- left
- turn
- straight

Discover

These are road signs. They tell people which way they need to turn.

Learn

You can use the words **left**, **right**, **clockwise** and **anticlockwise** to describe how you turn. Look at the hands on the clock.

Example

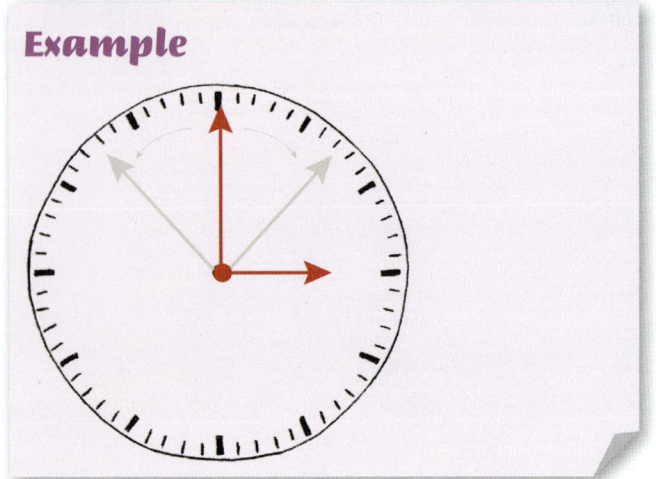

Lesson 3: **Square grids (1)**

- Find and describe a position on a grid

Key words
- row
- column
- grid
- position

Discover

You can see grids with squares in lots of different places.

Learn

You can use a grid of squares to name the position of an object.
Say the letter on the row first, then the number in the column.

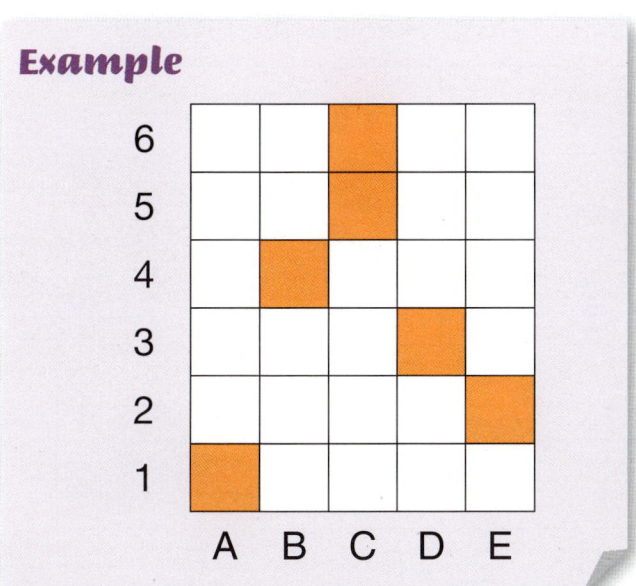

Example

A1

Geometry

Lesson 4: **Square grids (2)**

• Find and describe a position on a grid

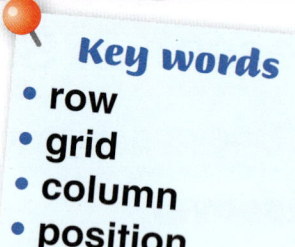

Key words
• row
• grid
• column
• position
• co-ordinate

Discover

This is a game that many people like to play. You have to use the labels on the rows and columns to work out the positions of different objects

Learn

Using labels on rows and columns can help you read maps.

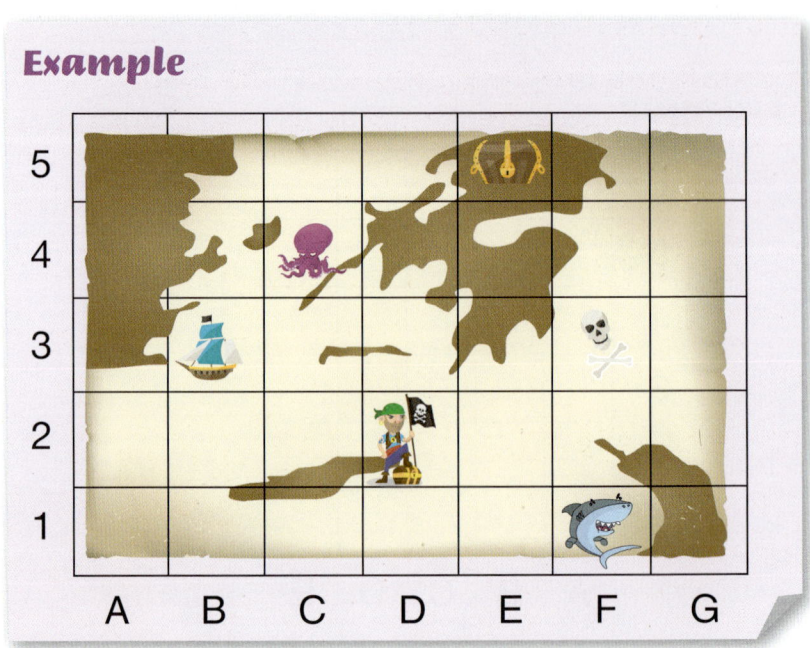

Example

Lesson 5: **Drawing right angles**

• Use a set square to draw right angles

Key words
• **right angle**
• **horizontal**
• **vertical**
• **perpendicular**
• **oblique**

Discover

What shapes can you see? Can you see any right angles?

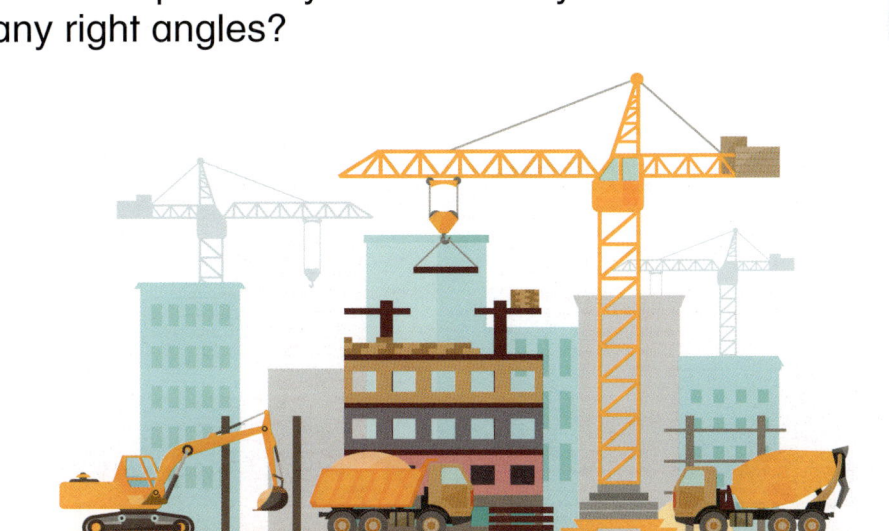

Learn

The right angles in the picture above are made from horizontal and vertical lines.

Sometimes they can be made from oblique lines. The lines that make a right angle are called **perpendicular**.

Example

Geometry

89

Lesson 6: **Comparing angles**

- Compare angles with right angles

Key words
- **right angle**
- **acute**
- **obtuse**

Discover

These flags have several things in common. What shapes can you see? Can you see any right angles?

Learn

You can compare right angles with other angles.

Angles can be smaller or larger than a right angle. Smaller angles are called **acute**. Larger angles are called **obtuse**.

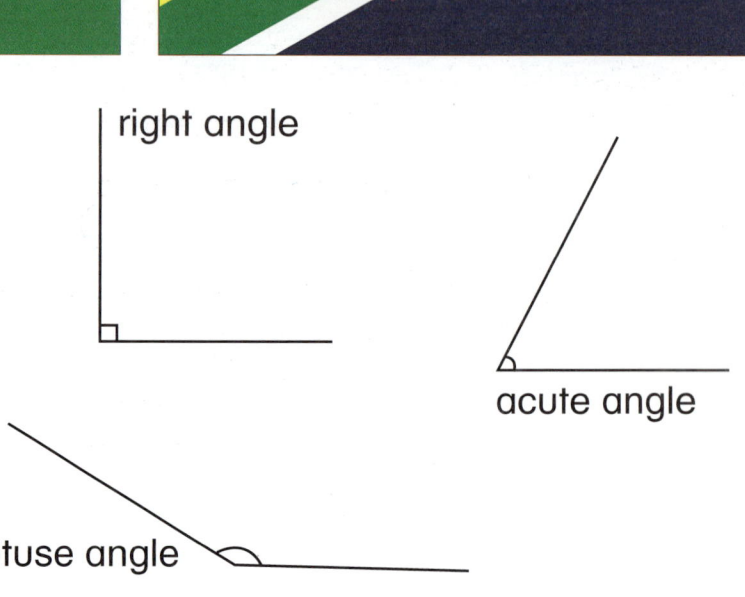

right angle

acute angle

obtuse angle

Example

Lesson 7: **Right angles and straight lines**

- Compare right angles with straight lines

Discover

The bird's wings can be at different angles. Can you see a right angle? Can you see any other angles?

Geometry

Learn

If you put two right angles side by side, you will get a straight line. A right angle is 90°, so a straight line must measure 180°.

Example

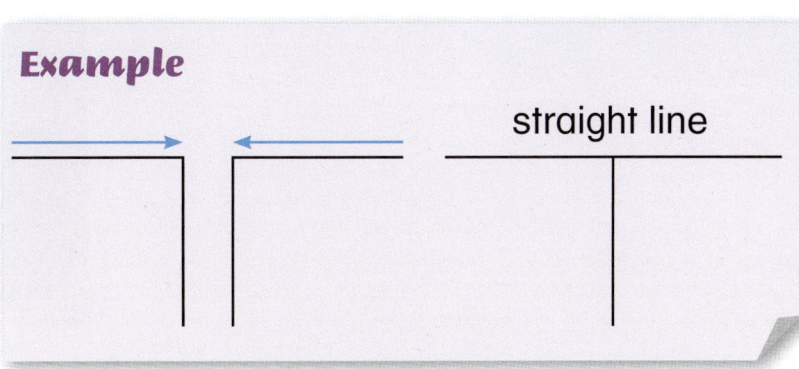

straight line

Lesson 8: **Angles are everywhere**

- Recognise angles in the world around us

Discover

What do you notice about the structures in the photographs? Can you see any angles? What shapes can you see?

Learn

Most structures in the world are made from shapes and angles.
Look for right angles and other angles that are smaller or larger. A building could be in the shape of a hexagon or an octagon.

Example

Lesson 1: **Notes and coins**

- Write money in the correct way

Discover

This money is the currency used by the USA. **Currency** is the word for the type of money a country uses.

Learn

There is a special way to write amounts of money. If there are 45 cents, you write 45c. If there are 445 cents, you write $4.45. You separate the whole dollars from the parts of a dollar with a decimal point.

Example

$	.		
4	.	4	5

Measure

93

Lesson 2: **Finding totals**

- Find totals of amounts of money

Key words
- note
- coin
- dollar
- total

Discover

This menu shows meals and side orders with their prices. Work out a meal that you would like to buy. How much is the total cost?

Rainbow restaurant

Pasta

	Regular	Large
Macaroni cheese	$3.55	$7.55
Spaghetti bolognese	$3.55	$7.55
Carbonara	$3.55	$7.55

Served with garlic bread.

Sides

	Small	Medium
Three bean salad	$1.45	$2.50
Tomato salsa	$1.45	$2.50
Leafy greens	$1.45	$2.50

Grilled

	Regular	Large
Grilled chicken	$5.80	$10.30
Tuna steak	$7.40	$11.50
Vegetable kebab	$4.75	$6.75

Served with potatoes.

Desserts

	2 scoops	4 scoops
Ice cream	75c	$1.20
Fruit salad	$2.25	
Banana sundae	$3.00	

Learn

You add amounts of money to find total costs. You can use facts and mental calculation strategies to do this. Rounding to the nearest dollar and adjusting is one of these strategies. Doubling is another. Use these to work out the cost of two regular grilled chicken meals.

Example
$5.80   Rounded: $6
$6 × 2 = $12
$12 − 40c = $11.60

Measure

Lesson 3: **Giving change**

- Find the coins and notes to make totals and give change

Discover

Toys can cost lots of different prices.
What is the cost of this car and teddy?

$48.75

$12.80

Learn

Use number facts and mental calculation strategies to add amounts of money and find total costs. To find change, count on from that total to the amount of money you have.

$12.80 is nearly $13.

Example

$13 − 20c = $12.80
$12.80 + 20c + $7 + $80 = $100
Change from $100 is $87.20.

Measure

Lesson 4: **Solving problems with money**

• Solve money problems by multiplying and halving

Discover

Can you name the different fruits and vegetables?
What do the price labels tell us?

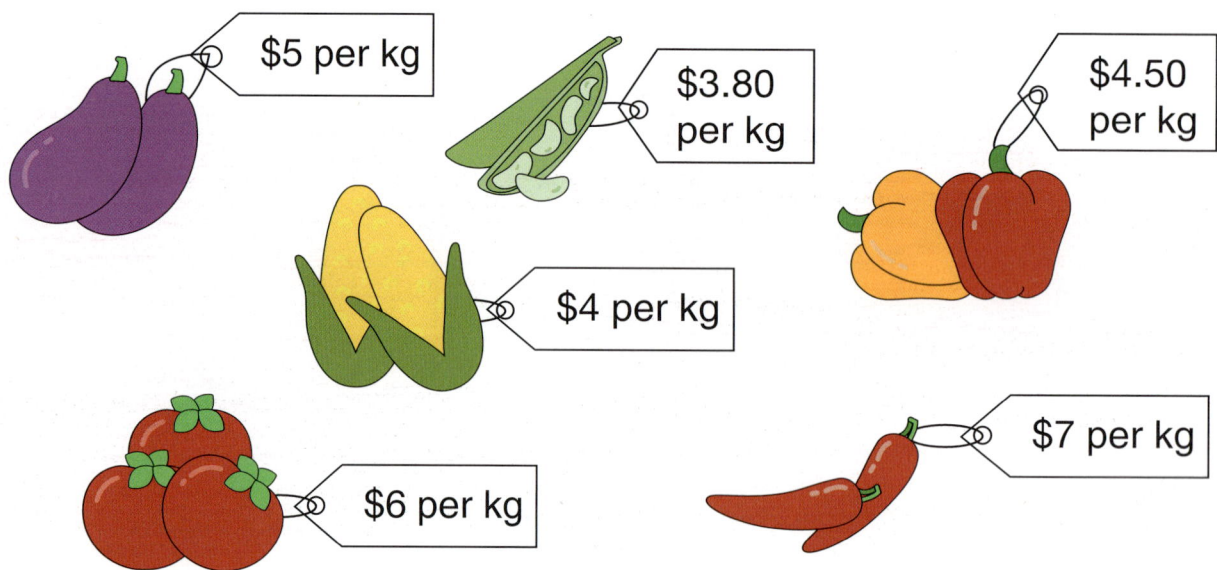

$5 per kg

$3.80 per kg

$4.50 per kg

$4 per kg

$7 per kg

$6 per kg

Learn

To buy half a kilogram of beans, halve the cost. To buy 4 times the amount of tomatoes, multiply the cost by 4.

Example
$3.80 ÷ 2 = $1.90
$6 × 4 = $24

What is half of $3.80?

96

Lesson 1: **Estimating, measuring and recording length**

- Choose and use units and equipment to measure length

Discover

This is a tennis court in a park. How many sections of the tennis court can you see? How would you measure the outside of each section to find out how long it is?

Learn

Use centimetres to measure short lengths, metres to measure longer lengths and kilometres to measure even longer lengths, called distance.

Example

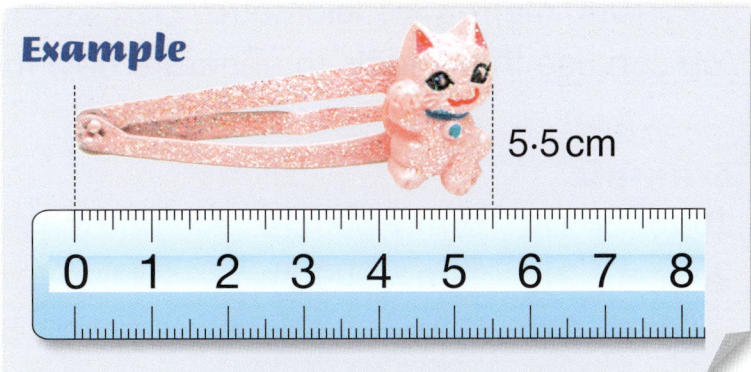

5·5 cm

Measure

Lesson 2: **Units of length**

- Convert between centimetres and metres, and metres and kilometres

Discover

This road goes through a rainforest in Brazil.
Which unit would you use to measure its length?

Learn

There is a relationship between centimetres, metres and kilometres.

- 100 centimetres = 1 metre
- 1000 metres = 1 kilometre

You can use these facts to generate new facts.

Example

100 cm = 1 m	5 m = 500 cm	1000 m = 1 km	7 km = 7000 m
200 cm = 2 m	9 m = 900 cm	4000 m = 4 km	10 km = 10 000 m
300 cm = 3 m	12 m = 1200 cm	8000 m = 8 km	6 km = 6000 m

Measure

Lesson 3: **Using a ruler**

- Draw and measure lines to the nearest centimetre with a ruler

Key words
- ruler
- centimetre (cm)
- nearest
- approximately

Discover

This lemur is the smallest primate in the world. Its body measures 6 cm. Its tail is about twice as long as its body.

Learn

Measure length by placing the zero on a ruler where you need to start measuring the object. Then, read the length on the ruler where the object ends.

Example

15 cm

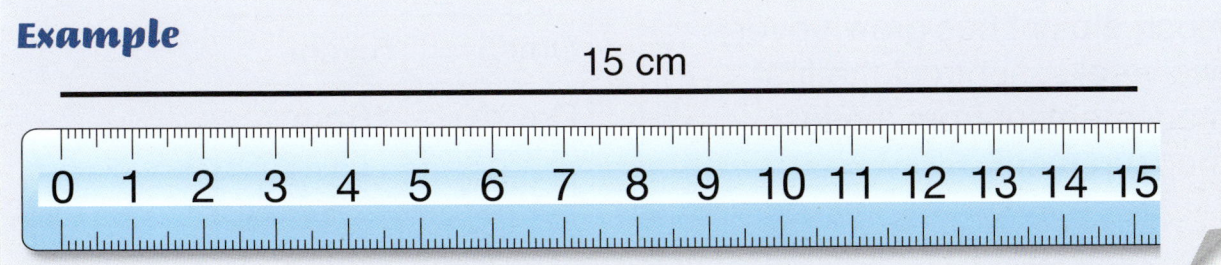

Measure

Lesson 4: **Solving problems involving length**

- Solve word problems involving length

Key words
- length
- height
- width
- centimetre (cm)
- metre (m)
- kilometre (km)

Discover

You can measure plants to see how well they are growing. Recording the measurements helps scientists to find the best conditions for them to grow.

Learn

You can solve problems involving length by calculating. For example, to work out how much a plant has grown over two weeks, subtract the first measurement from the last measurement.

Example

Height of plant in centimetres

Day 1	3 cm
Day 5	$5\frac{1}{2}$ cm
Day 10	16 cm
Day 14	$22\frac{1}{2}$ cm

Lesson 1: **Estimating, measuring and recording mass**

Key words
• kilogram (kg)
• gram (g)
• heavy
• light
• balance
• scales

• Choose and use units and equipment to measure mass

Discover

You could weigh lots of different things on these scales. Which one would be used to weigh you?

Learn

Use grams to measure the mass of small objects and kilograms to measure the mass of heavier objects. You can use different types of scale to measure different things.

Example

kilograms   grams

Measure

101

Lesson 2: **Units of mass**

- Convert between grams and kilograms, and kilograms and grams

Discover

This is a Fennec fox. It lives in North Africa and can have a mass of up to 1·6 kg. Which of the weights shown are equivalent to this mass?

Learn

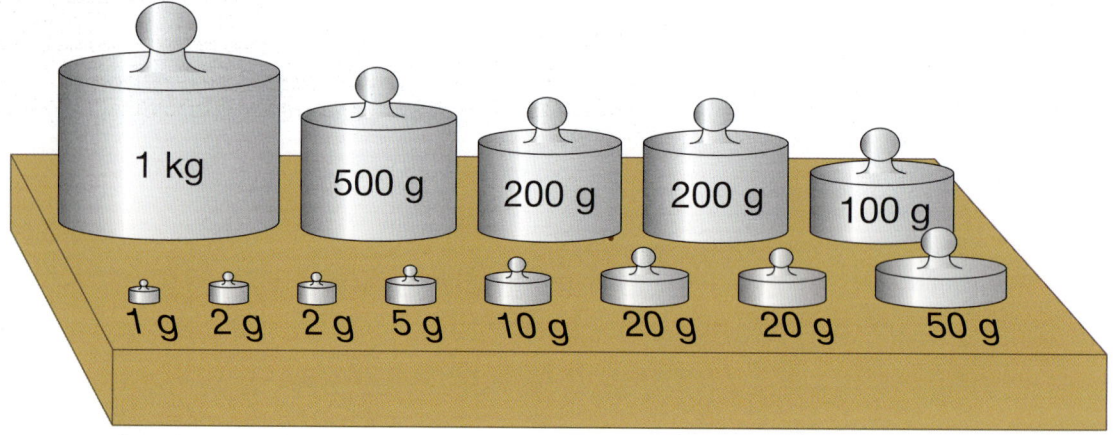

1000 grams are equivalent to one kilogram. We can use strategies such as doubling and halving to find equivalences.

Example

1000 g = 1 kg	6 kg = 6000 g
2000 g = 2 kg	3 kg = 3000 g
4000 g = 4 kg	$1\frac{1}{2}$ kg = 1500 g

Measure

Lesson 3: **Using scales**

• Read the mass of objects using scales

Key words
• **scales**
• **kilograms (kg)**
• **grams (g)**
• **nearest**
• **approximately**

Discover

The apple is on a digital scale.
How heavy is the apple?

Learn

To measure mass, place an object on a scale and look at where the needle is pointing. That tells you the mass. This could be on, or near, a whole number of kilograms or a division between kilograms.

Example

Measure

Lesson 4: **Solving problems involving mass**

- Solve word problems involving mass

Discover

What is the man on the market stall doing?

Learn

You can solve problems involving mass.
Problems will also include calculating.

Example

You can use models to help solve problems.

Sarah needs 5 kg of rice to prepare a meal. She has 2 kg 750 g of rice. How much more rice does she need?

5 kg	
2 kg 750 g	g?

You can count back from 5 kg to 2 kg 750 g, or count on from 2 kg 750 g to 5 kg. Which is easier?

Measure

Lesson 1: **Estimating, measuring and recording capacity**

- Choose and use units and equipment to measure capacity

Key words
- litres (*l*)
- millilitres (ml)
- measuring vessel
- interval

Discover

Measuring spoons can measure small amounts of liquid. How many millilitres can these spoons hold?

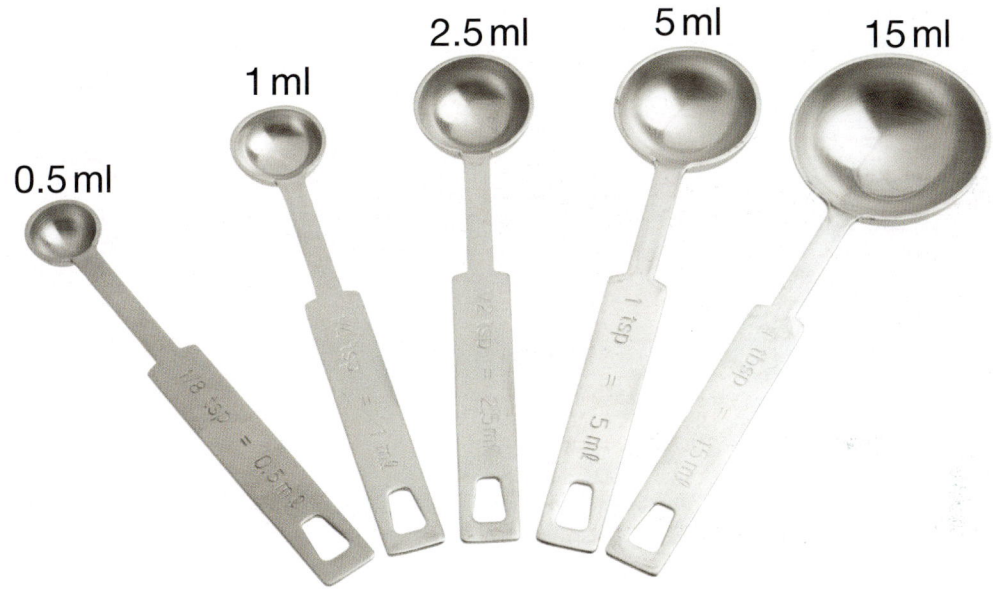

0.5 ml   1 ml   2.5 ml   5 ml   15 ml

Learn

Measuring jugs can measure capacity and volume, using millilitres for small amounts and litres for greater amounts. The largest volume this jug can measure is 1 litre.

Example

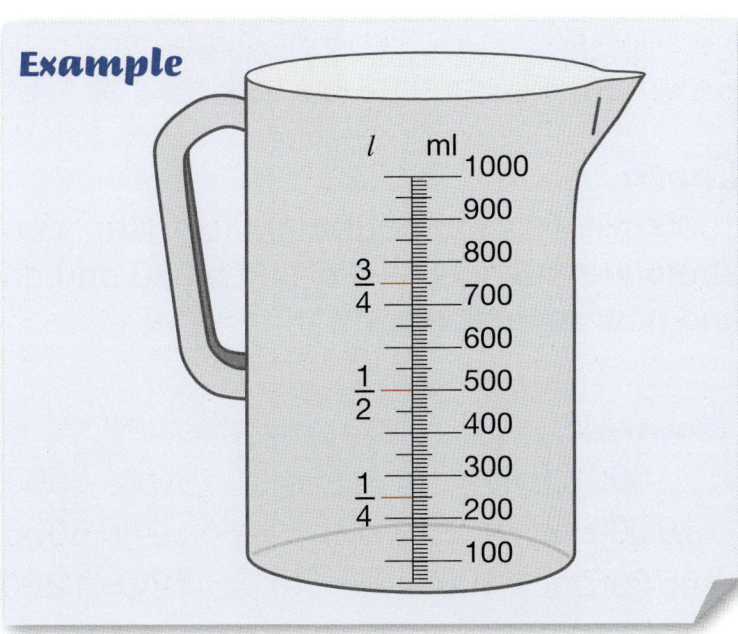

l   ml
1000
900
800
¾ — 700
600
½ — 500
400
¼ — 300
200
100

Measure

Lesson 2: **Units of capacity**

- Convert between millilitres and litres, and litres and millilitres

Discover

These containers hold different amounts of liquid. The capacity of the largest bottle is 2 litres. What do you think are the capacities of the other containers?

Learn

1000 millilitres are equivalent to 1 litre. You can use strategies such as multiplying by 10 and dividing to find new equivalences.

Example

1000 ml = 1 *l*	3 *l* = 3000 ml
10 000 ml = 10 *l*	6 *l* = 6000 ml
100 000 ml = 100 *l*	12 *l* = 12 000 ml

Measure

Lesson 3: **Using measuring vessels**

- Read capacity using the scale on measuring vessels

Discover

What is this container for?
How would you use it?

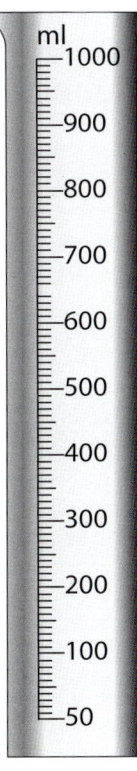

Learn

You can measure capacity or volume by pouring liquid into a container. You then read the scale where the liquid stops. This could be on, or near, a whole number of litres or a division between litres.

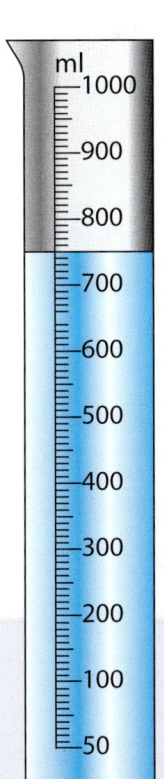

Example

By reading the scale, you can see the volume of liquid in the measuring cylinder is 750 ml.

Measure

Lesson 4: **Solving problems involving capacity**

- Solve word problems involving capacity

Discover

In this milkshake bar, the shakes are sold in half litre or litre glasses. What size milkshake do you think the girls are drinking?

Learn

You can use strategies that you know to solve problems involving capacity.

Example

Sylvie makes 25 half litre shakes and 13 one litre shakes. How much milk does she need altogether?

$25 \times 500 \, ml = 12\,500 \, ml$

$12\,500 \, ml \quad = 12\frac{1}{2} \, l$

$12\frac{1}{2} + 13 \quad = 25\frac{1}{2} \, l$

Sylvie needs $25\frac{1}{2}$ litres of milk.

Measure

Lesson 1: **Units of time**

Key words
- **time**
- **second**
- **minute**
- **hour**
- **day**
- **week**

- Choose and use units to measure time

Discover

This instrument measures short lengths of time. Do you know what it is? When do you think one of these might be used?

Learn

You use analogue or digital clocks and watches to tell the time. Sometimes these show seconds. There are 60 seconds in a minute. 60 minutes are equivalent to 1 hour and 24 hours are equivalent to 1 day.

You can work out other equivalences using mental calculation strategies.

Measure

Example

60 seconds	=	1 minute
120 seconds	=	2 minutes
600 seconds	=	10 minutes
30 seconds	=	$\frac{1}{2}$ minute
150 seconds	=	$2\frac{1}{2}$ minutes

Lesson 2: **Telling the time**

• Tell the time on analogue and digital clocks

Key words
• time
• analogue
• digital
• minutes past
• minutes to

Discover

This is the world's largest clock. It is in Saudi Arabia. How is it the same as other clocks? How is it different?

Measure

Example

Learn

You can tell the time by finding the minutes past an hour. This clock shows 35 minutes past 9 o'clock. The equivalent digital time is 9:35. There are 25 minutes until the next hour. So, it is 25 minutes to 10 o'clock.

Lesson 3: **Calculating time intervals**

• Calculate time intervals in hours and minutes

Discover

Some activities take a long time to do, some take a short time.

Does it take hours or minutes to get ready for school?

Learn

You can use a number line to find time intervals in hours and minutes.

Measure

> ### Example
>
> Jebede's swimming lesson started at 4:45 and ended at 5:35.
> How long was her lesson?
>
> Start at 4:45, count on 15 minutes to 5:00 then 35 minutes to 5:35.
>
> 15 minutes   35 minutes
>
> 4:45   5:00   5:35
>
> The length of Jebede's swimming lesson was 50 minutes.

Lesson 4: **Reading a calendar**

- Read a calendar and calculate intervals in weeks or days

Discover

This smartphone calendar shows all the days in August 2016. How many days are there in August?

Learn

Calendars help you to plan your time and remember special occasions, like birthdays. You find time intervals by counting on weeks and days.

Example

You can work out what day it will be 2 weeks and 3 days after the 4th of the month.

Sunday	Monday	Tuesday	Wednesday	Thursday	Friday	Saturday
	1	2	3	4	5	6
7	8	9	10	11	12	13
14	15	16	17	18	19	20
21	22	23	24	25	26	27
28	29	30	31			

AUGUST 2016

Measure

Lesson 1: **Charts and tables**

- Record information in charts and tables and interpret them

Key words
- tally
- tally chart
- frequency table
- information

Discover

What different animals can you see in the pictures? You can use tally charts and frequency tables to record the number of each type of animal.

Learn

In a tally chart, each item is recorded with a line. The fifth item in each group is shown using a diagonal line.

You can show the information from a tally chart in a table.

Example

lions	|||
giraffes	##+
elephants	##+ |||
zebras	##+	

Animal	Number
lions	3
giraffes	5
elephants	8
zebras	6

Handling data

Lesson 2: **Pictograms**

- Show and describe information on a pictogram

Discover

Which fruits can you identify? Which of these fruits do you eat?

Learn

You can find out the most popular fruits in the class by making a list and a tally. You can then represent this information in a pictogram.

Example

This pictogram shows how many bananas were eaten over a week.

Bananas eaten

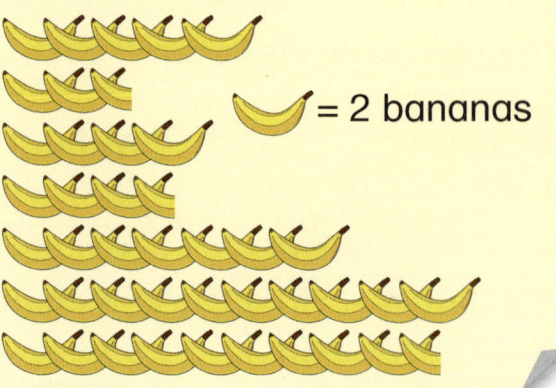

Monday	
Tuesday	
Wednesday	
Thursday	
Friday	
Saturday	
Sunday	

= 2 bananas

Handling data

Lesson 3: **Bar charts**

- Show and describe information on a bar chart

Key words
- bar chart
- intervals
- vertical axis
- represent
- information

Discover
Can you play any of these musical instruments?

Learn
You can use a bar chart to represent information. Bar charts have a vertical axis that can go up in divisions of 1 or 2.

Example
There are 4 kiwis, 8 apples, 6 bananas and 2 dragonfruit represented on this bar chart.

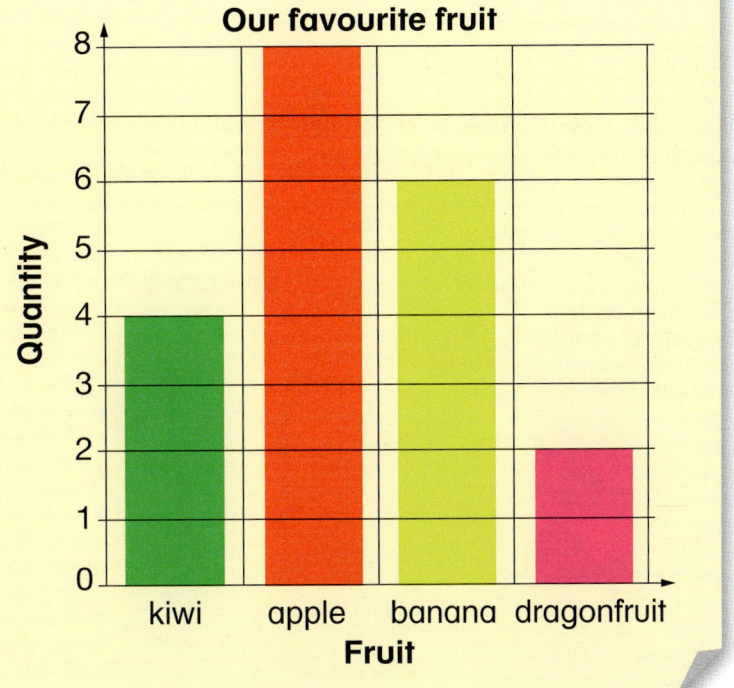

Our favourite fruit

Handling data

115

Lesson 4: **Venn diagrams**

• Use a Venn diagram to sort data and objects

Discover

How many of these shapes can you name? How could you sort them?

Learn

You can sort the shapes into a Venn diagram. A Venn diagram shows properties that are different and properties that are the same.

Example

The shapes go in the Venn diagram under the headings 'Flat faces', 'Curved surfaces' or in the intersection.

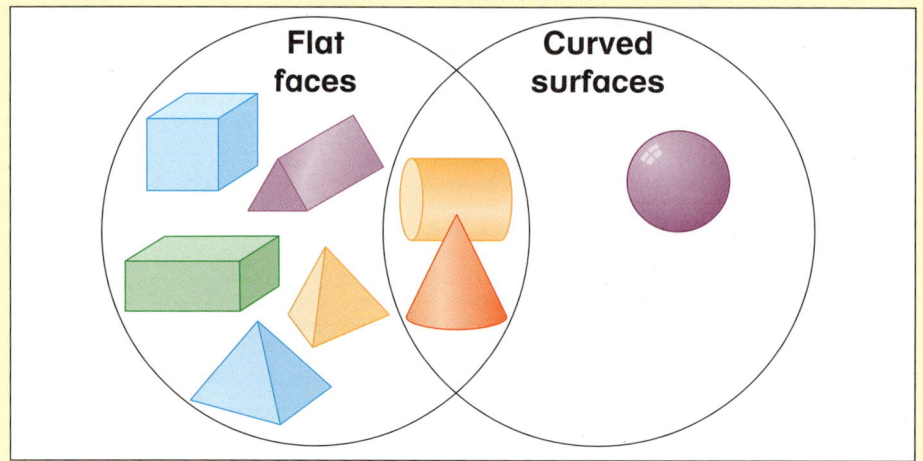

Flat faces   Curved surfaces

Handling data

116

Lesson 5: **Carroll diagrams**

- Use a Carroll diagram to sort data and objects

Key words
- Carroll diagram
- sort
- data
- objects
- criteria

Discover

What animals are these? Can you describe them? Where do they live?

Learn

You have learned how to sort using a Venn diagram.
You can also sort using a Carroll diagram.
A Carroll diagram sorts things according to a criteria and not that criteria.

Example

You can sort the animals into the Carroll diagram below.

	Legs	No legs
Lives in the sea	crab	fish
Does not live in the sea	lion	snake

Handling data

Lesson 6: **Using charts and tables**

- Collect, organise and interpret data using tally charts and frequency tables

Discover

Many schools offer three different lunch options.

Learn

To help answer questions, you can collect, organise and interpret information using tally charts and frequency tables.

You can show how many learners have each type of lunch.

Example

How many learners have school dinners, packed lunch, or go home?

school dinner   ⅏⅏ ⅏⅏ ||
packed lunch   ⅏⅏ ⅏⅏ ⅏⅏
home ||||

Lunch type	Number
school dinner	12
packed lunch	15
home	4

Lesson 7: **Using pictograms and bar charts**

- Collect, organise and interpret data using pictograms and bar charts

Discover

Learners travel to school in different ways.
How do you travel to school?

Learn

Many schools take surveys of how learners travel to school. They often do this to answer questions to do with road safety or traffic.

Example
How do learners travel to school?

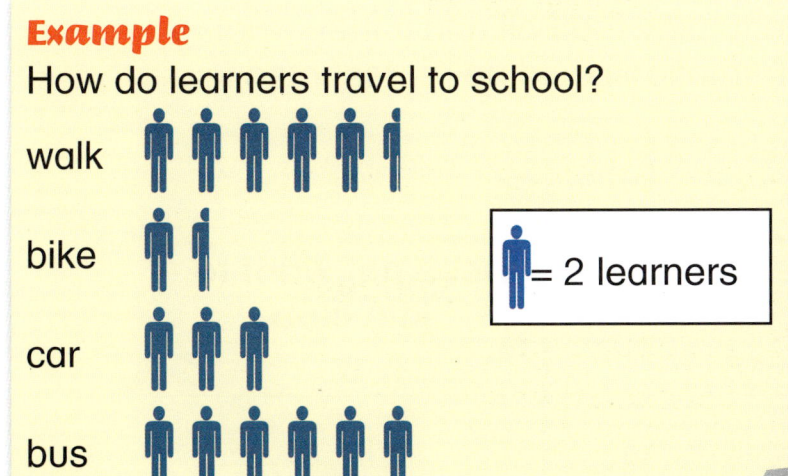

= 2 learners

Handling data

Lesson 8: Using Venn and Carroll diagrams

- Collect, organise and interpret data using Venn and Carroll diagrams

Discover

Learn

If a PE teacher wanted to organise a football club, they would need to know if learners like to play football and if they want to join the club, or not. The information could be represented in a Venn or Carroll diagram.

Example

	Wants to join club	Does not want to join club
Plays football	18	6
Does not play football	2	10

Handling data

Notes

Notes

Notes

Photo acknowledgements

Every effort has been made to trace copyright holders.

Any omission will be rectified at the first opportunity.

Front cover and title page Jose Lis Petaez/Getty Images, p1l Hirurg/Shutterstock, p1c Rafael Croonen/Shutterstock, p1r holdeneye/Shutterstock, p2 La Gorda/Shutterstock, p11 (grasshopper) Sujono sujono/Shutterstock, p14t alexsvirid/Shutterstock, p15l Jim Barber/Shutterstock, p15r Chris W. Anderson/Shutterstock, p16t aperturesound/Shutterstock, p16b Luis Louro/Shutterstock, p17 (both) Visual Generation/Shutterstock, p18 Worldpics/Shutterstock, p19 Nelson Marques/Shutterstock, p20 oldmonk/Shutterstock, p21 BlueSkyImage/Shutterstock, p22l Albo003/Shutterstock, p22r Roman Samokhin/Shutterstock, p23 Lukas Gojda/Shutterstock, p24b wanpatsorn/Shutterstock, p25 Stephen Rees/Shutterstock, p26l, r Viktor1/Shutterstock, p26c M. Unal Ozmen/Shutterstock, p27 TasfotoNL/Shutterstock, p28 Picsfive/Shutterstock, p29 Vanatchanan/Shutterstock, p35 Sergiy Kuzmin/Shutterstock, p38 michaeljung/Shutterstock, p40l James Clarke/Shutterstock, p40r and b mayakova/Shutterstock, p41 (both) Visual Generation/Shutterstock, p44 Niloo/Shutterstock, p48 Yu Zhang/Shutterstock, p49 bbay/Shutterstock, p51 James Clarke/Shutterstock, p55 michaeljung/Shutterstock, p58 marinini/Shutterstock, p59 Mata Vector/Shutterstock, p60 Prezoom.nl/Shutterstock, p69 Ivonne Wierink/Shutterstock, p71tl M. Unal Ozmen/Shutterstock, p71cl and cr mihalec/Shutterstock, p71tr M. Unal Ozmen/Shutterstock, p71bl tanuha2001/Shutterstock, p71br oksana2010/Shutterstock, p74l Vorobyeva/Shutterstock, p74r wavebreakmedia/Shutterstock, p75tl DVARG/Shutterstock, p75tr Ekarin Apirakthanakorn/Shutterstock, p75bl Smileus/Shutterstock, p75bcl a6photo/Shutterstock, p75bcr Dan Thornberg/Shutterstock, p75br TRINACRIA PHOTO/Shutterstock, p77l Everett Historical/Shutterstock, p77r Radu Bercan/Shutterstock, p78tl anaken2012/Shutterstock, p78tr Aratehortua/Shutterstock, p78bl HeinzTeh/Shutterstock, p78br anaken2012/Shutterstock, p79tl EKS/Shutterstock, p79cl Mega Pixel/Shutterstock, p79cr Paul Velgos/Shutterstock, p79br Kamolrat/Shutterstock, p80l BOONCHUAY PROMJIAM/Shutterstock, p80c Migelito/Shutterstock, p80r Janis Smits/Shutterstock, p81 hecke61/Shutterstock, p82 PinkBlue/Shutterstock, p84tl sspopov/Shutterstock, p84tcl Designsstock/Shutterstock, p84tcr Duplass/Shutterstock, p84tr Natan86/Shutterstock, p84cl Matthew Cole/Shutterstock, p84cr Smileus/Shutterstock, p84b Ivonne Wierink/Shutterstock, p85 Africa Studio/Shutterstock, p86l binik/Shutterstock, p86r Nicola Renna/Shutterstock, p87l Jne Valokuvaus/Shutterstock, p87r edography/Shutterstock, p89 theromb/Shutterstock, p91t Sekar B/Shutterstock, p91b Wollertz/Shutterstock, p92tl Oliver Foerstner/Shutterstock, p92tr StevenRussellSmithPhotos/Shutterstock, p92br Route66/Shutterstock, p93 (notes) Mr. High Sky/Shutterstock, p93 (coins) Vladimir Wrangel/Shutterstock, p94tl Brent Hofacker/Shutterstock, p94tr Louella938/Shutterstock, p94bl Jacek Chabraszewski/Shutterstock, p94br annata78/Shutterstock, p95tl Audrius Merfeldas/Shutterstock, p95tr Valentina Proskurina/Shutterstock, p97t Blanscape/Shutterstock, p97b Pavel V Mukhin/Shutterstock, p98 Dr. Morley Read/Shutterstock, p99 David Thyberg/Shutterstock, p100 oliveromg/Shutterstock, p101l kulyk/Shutterstock, p101c graphixmania/Shutterstock, p101r ayzek/Shutterstock, p102tl Dmitry Kovtun/Shutterstock, p102tr nattanan726/Shutterstock, p103 Gtranquillity/Shutterstock, p104 paul prescott/Shutterstock, p105 Hurst Photo/Shutterstock, p106 dimair/Shutterstock, p108 stockyimages/Shutterstock, p109 Stepan Bormotov/Shutterstock, p110 rasoulali/Shutterstock, p111 wavebreakmedia/Shutterstock, p112 Fenton one/Shutterstock, p113tl Pearl Media/Shutterstock, p113tr Denise Thompson/Shutterstock, p113bl Johan Swanepoel/Shutterstock, p113br Villiers Steyn/Shutterstock, p114 Denis Vrublevski/Shutterstock, p115 Elena Schweitzer/Shutterstock, p117tl Ozgur Coskun/Shutterstock, p117c blackboard1965/Shutterstock, p117r Eric Isselee/Shutterstock, p117bl Brilliance stock/Shutterstock, p118l Mike Flippo/Shutterstock, p118c www.BillionPhotos/Shutterstock, p118r wckiw/Shutterstock, p119tl Mike Focus/Shutterstock, p119tr Ljupco Smokovski/Shutterstock, p119br ChristineGonsalves/Shutterstock, p120 AGIF/Shutterstock.